The
MOMOLOGUE
Collective

AN ANTHOLOGY BY SELF-IDENTIFYING MOTHERS

GATHERED BY BRIANNA M. ALLEN

Self-published by Brianna Allen.

A grateful acknowledgment to the participants and contributors to The Momologue Collective. www.MomologueCollective.com

ISBN 979-8-9867031-0-7 (paperback)
ISBN 979-8-9867031-1-4 (ebook)

Printed in the United States.

Cover Design by Kammi Matson.

ACKNOWLEDGMENTS

My deepest thanks to the 82 story-tellers
who created this collection of 100 Momologues.
You came when I needed community.
You became the community.
We created this space, side-by-side.

Thank you Mercedes O'Leary for your supreme devotion to each storyteller's voice, and for neighborhood walks of encouragement.

Dearest Carla Klinker Cope, Amy Komar, Amy Meissner, Somer Hahm, Myesha Callahan Freet and Lily Hope, Thank you for your care and courage as Artist/Mothers.

Thank you Kammi Matson for always enthusiastically saying "Yes!" to collaboration.

Thank you Amanda Benwell, Adele Person, Miranda Weiss, Jennifer Norton, Dorothy Duncan and Bianca van der Meulen.

A special thank you to Melissa Jackson-Shuck, whose heart and generosity made this book possible.

Published with support from Pier One Theatre, Homer, Alaska, Thank You!

ARTIST'S NOTE

"Art is a good way to recognize oneself."

— LOUISE BOURGEOIS

Within the first month of her life, my daughter completely rewired my brain. I didn't recognize myself inside or out. My family was across the country, my husband was out at sea. I was primarily alone for the first 6 months of her life — living in a lofted-cabin, high-summer in the land of the midnight sun.

By the time I was pregnant again (sooner than planned) and now with a wild, soon-to-be toddler, I needed community. I couldn't paint, but I could listen and feel connected to many. A community began to emerge. My art practice evolved.

The Momologue Collective is a catalyst for my artwork, whether painting or performance or other, and ignites me with vigor and bravery. These storytellers make me feel safe and supported when I look inward at myself—both as a mother and as an artist. May we lift women's voices and embolden new artwork, hand in hand.

I am forever grateful for the gift of collaboration
and the generous, brave voices here.
My Best, Brianna

EDITOR'S NOTE

"I have never told anyone," says a mom in this collection.

So it was with the greatest delicacy that I approached editing, driven to uphold the integrity of the mothers' voices. At times I fretted over the most basic of edits out of determination to not change a woman's perspective, sensibilities, or experience.

Each of these Momologues holds one great truth: every woman is the expert of her own life.

These mothers know what they need to mother. They reckon with choices they never knew they had, or maybe don't have. None of these mothers parent from a place of equity. They get what they get. They do their best and beyond, and they sometimes still feel like failures.

We often think of choice, especially now, in terms of abortion rights. But "choice" is a theme broader and more complicated than conception and conceiving.

These mothers show us the emotional realities of having choice undermined by both nature and society. In the Momologues, women navigate fertility struggles. Perfectly planned labors go awry. Women are given medicine they don't want and can't get medicine they request. They don't get to choose when they sleep, wake, or eat: the demands of caring for a baby and children far exceed what they expected. Often, motherhood is also better than they expected too: love overwhelms in ways they couldn't have anticipated.

There is grief. Children aren't always who we expect them to be. Sometimes we fail them. Sometimes children die. Sometimes mothers die. Sometimes the gap between what we expected and how life turns out is so great that we don't know how to move forward.

And where are the partners? Sometimes there. Sometimes not. The women in these stories can name what they need, but that doesn't mean they get it. As one mom says, "My husband got to choose whether to sleep in or stay up late, but my exhausted body didn't have a choice."

These mostly anonymous narratives are not so anonymous, in the sense that we recognize ourselves, our friends, our neighbors, our sisters, our mothers, our co-workers—we recognize each other and the grind and delight of bearing and raising humans.

One recent morning, I left the house to go for a walk. My kids, 8 and 11, were acting like kids and I needed space. My mind was full of adult needs that would most likely be put on the back burner for the rest of the day. It all felt like too much, even though on the surface everything was okay. Brianna saw me walking down the road and slowed her car to say hi. My composure cracked and I teared up and said, "It just feels like everything I do is invisible," then a car pulled behind her so she drove away.

When I got home from my walk, there was a bouquet picked from her garden with a note, "I see you."

This collection is about being seen; about acknowledging the hardest truths non-judgmentally. This collaboration of 82 mother writers, plus mother editors and creators and designers, reveals what we already instinctually knew: women mother the world and deliver each other.

- Mercedes O'Leary

"We need to make chosen families of small groups of women who support each other, talk to each other regularly, can speak their truths and their experiences, and find they're not alone in them. It makes all the difference."

— GLORIA STEINEM

———— • ————

TABLE OF CONTENTS

WELCOME

As it began, The Momologue Collective collected stories about pregnancy, labor, birth, motherhood, and parenting to shed light on the more surprising, defeating, and hilarious moments we never saw coming.

While these particular stories were amassed between October 2019 - July 2022, two major events happened: First, the Covid-19 global pandemic was declared on March 11th, 2020 and second, the U.S. Supreme court overturned Roe v. Wade on June 25th, 2022.

Naturally, new and returning contributors responded accordingly– By gifting their most tender stories in the face of adversity. One contributor writes "It seems society has this impossible expectation of women to work as if we don't have children and to mother as if we don't have work." Corporate America's exploitation of women, mothers, and minorities has always been fundamental to it's success. Gender gaps, wealth and racial inequities prevail and ironically, we all are expected to be grateful for such a standard of "freedom."

The stories built a cross-continental community for all women to mourn a monumental loss of one's choice to become a mother at all. It became evident that stories about access and choice are fundamental to our collective American mothering experience.

This anthology offers a critical look at how American motherhood feels for mothers and womxn from the inside out; It's a refreshing, unapologetically feminine compilation written by strangers, but read like a diary.

As these stories are read, one can sense how feminism is evolving dynamically, and for that I am hopeful.

Thank you for being here.

WRITE A MOMOLOGUE

The Momologue Collective welcomes self-identifying mothers to contribute to a growing anthology of voices. Combined voices provide context for wider narratives. This is important. You are important. Share your surprise, your defeat, your battle and your victory as long days become short years. Commemorate your experience by participating in this exchange, and become something bigger, together.

Looking forward, The Momologue Collective aims to house bona fide truths by self-identifying mothers among more vulnerable subjects like race, privilege, gender bias, fertility, puberty, neurodivergence, gun-control, atypical family structures, socio-economic status, and death. Motherhood changes but it's always a powerful common denominator among the most delicate and polarized places.

Here, you are safe to explore your mother edges.

Join in the collective by contributing a story at

www.MomologueCollective.com

ANONYMITY

Anonymity is essential to provide a protected, judgment-free space to share. While the majority of authors wish to remain anonymous, a few share their first name at the closing.

———— ● ————

Your trust is the biggest gift of all.
We are doing good work together.

VOLUME ONE

IT'S TIME

"Remember our heritage is our power;

we can know ourselves and our

capacities by seeing that other women

have been strong."

—Judy Chicago

———— • ————

INCOMPETENT CERVIX

Five days after my due date, there was still no baby, no effacement, and I was not dilated at all. Being diagnosed with an "incompetent cervix" was depressing and defeating. Like, how the fuck can a cervix be incompetent?! Who coined that term? It felt pretty crappy, to say the least. Yes, I had a pretty traumatic birth experience, followed by a NICU stay after my first pregnancy. But baby number two was a breeze — I didn't even have to work or try to birth her. So much for incompetent, huh?

I'VE SEEN WORSE

My dad's Alzheimer's was ramping up when I was pregnant with my daughter. When I went into labor, he insisted on being there, even though every once in a while, you could tell he wasn't sure who I was. He walked me around the maternity ward — an endless loop — like a champ. He also got a full front stage view of me having a catheter put in. He demanded I get an epidural because he had heard me beg for one. When it was over — **and he had seen the whole thing** — I apologized, and he said, "I've seen worse!" We both laughed, and I cried a bit. He was the first person to hold my daughter when she was born, as I was in recovery from the C-section. I will never, ever forget those moments — I was lucky to have them.

TERRIFIED I WOULDN'T RECOGNIZE MY OWN CHILD

Right after my daughter was born they took her to the nursery; cleaned me up, and moved me from the birthing room to a regular room. As they wheeled me past the nursery, I was suddenly terrified I wouldn't recognize my own child. The moment I saw her, I knew how crazy of a thought that was!

WHAT THEY COULDN'T TELL ME

No one can tell you what it will be like to be ten days overdue, lost in a hazy world of anxiety and anticipation, wanting to finally see your baby's face, wanting it to be over, wanting so much to have your story to tell. No one can tell you what it will feel like, after almost a full day of labor, to have your arms strapped down and your glasses removed. To be martyred and sacrificed on the surgery table, blind and feverish, and to hear your baby pulled from your belly with a great sucking noise. To hear her cry for the first time, of many many times, and to cry your own tears, your belly empty and detached and very far away.

No one can tell you that you will lie in the hospital bed on IV antibiotics, enjoying your catheter, blissfully unaware, that as your body molds itself around your new precious child, an infection is incubating in your gut, so that by the time you are home, your husband is back at work, and people have visited and said farewell, that you will shit mucus and water for weeks, months, for so long that your sisters will whisper behind your back, jealous of your lost baby weight, but you will still, still, still be nursing your child, giving her everything that you manage to keep, and everything that YOU no longer have.

No one can tell you what the second child will do to you. They can't.

They can't tell you that even though you are determined not to have another C-section, you make the appointment anyway. They don't tell you that you will go into labor only after you give up control and realize, deep down, that you never had any control to begin with.

They can't tell you that the second child will come so quickly that you will pee all over the passenger seat of the car, on your hands and knees, and want to start pushing there in the hospital parking lot. They can't tell you that you will strip completely naked as soon as you enter the birthing room and how you will be only mildly aware of all the people around you, poking an IV into your hand, telling you to push, then not to push.

They can't tell you that you will think, "This isn't so bad," but you won't want to say it out loud in case you jinx yourself. They can't tell you what it's like to get impatient with pushing, or what it's like to give birth squatting, or to see your own deep red blood flowing down your legs and over your tiny monkey baby's body. To climb into the bed, deliver a placenta, ask for a hamburger and a milkshake and feel high. Not blissfully high, but kind of crazy, selfish high.

They don't tell you that the VBAC will be so hard to recover from, that every time you sit down to pee, it will feel like your most private and discreet parts are falling out. They will look like badly butchered meat for long after the six-week mark — when most people have healed enough to have sex again — but you will LAUGH at the thought.

They don't tell you that your second child will maybe break you and your family. This beautiful alien will be so tuned into her wild toddler sister that she will barely nurse, and she will be swimming in circles at 2 months, and that by the time you realize that she isn't gaining weight, you will know it's all your fault. For being distracted; for feeling too confident.

They don't tell you that each child is so different that everything you thought you knew won't apply and you will have to negotiate a brand new understanding of how to live.

They don't tell you any of this.

They ask, "Are you so happy?" and "Are you getting any sleep?"

"Yes," you answer truthfully.

And "It's fine," even though it's not, and because it is.

MOMMA BEAR AND NIPPLE STIMULATION

With my second child, my water broke nine days early with the full moon, so baby was not really in any mood to join us but we needed to get baby moving regardless. When the nurses started to threaten me with an IV and Pitocin about twelve hours later, it was time for Momma Bear to take matters into her own hands. Like my first baby, this was going to be all-natural. I remember thinking, while they were discussing what to do, **that they didn't know who they were messing with**. This birth was going to be under my terms, not theirs. It's pretty amazing the type of movement some good ole nipple stimulation can create. Once things got serious, baby joined us in about an hour. He came so fast that he almost slipped right through the midwife's hands. Don't mess with Momma Bear. My body was made for this.

ANTICIPATION

My first baby woke me up in the middle of the night. Woke dad up too; we were excited and nervous! There were no cell phones back then, so in anticipation of making the phone call announcement, dad knew he needed change to make a pay phone call.

We had collected change, like many did, in a large glass water jug. Before I knew it, he had emptied the entire container on top of a table saw we had set up in the living room, as we were in the middle of renovations.

We laughed so hard. All we needed were a couple of dimes.

POOP

My husband promised not to tell me if I pooped during labor. Of course, I asked him anyway. He just stared at me — terrified.

"Raising a family wasn't something I put on my resumé, but I have to ask myself, would I apply for the same job again?"

– ERMA BOMBECK

———— • ————

THE DAY HE DIDN'T SHOW UP

This is about the day my husband forgot to show up. The day I gave birth to my second child. He showed up in body, in his handsome male form, but not in the way that mattered. And I was not prepared.

There was no reason for me to think he was going to half-ass it this time. I still remember the first time — how he stood by my side during most of my thirty-hour labor, and how his eyes filled with the perfect amount of worry, wonder, calm, and excitement. Afterward, he changed diapers, fed me, held the baby, cooed, and said adorable things like, "Don't worry I won't let anyone spank you!" We discussed swaddling techniques, argued about when to introduce a pacifier, and totally nailed the sleep training as a team. We were happy.

But this story is not about that time, it's about the second time, my second childbirth, which at least, went a lot quicker. From the time my pains began to "I don't want my 4-year-old son to see me like this," was only about an hour or two. I retreated to my bedroom to gather myself and gear up for round two. My husband followed me. I was on my yoga mat panting and moaning, and he was sitting on the bed with his phone, giving me little peeks but not seeming too interested.

"Can you help me count my contractions?" I asked.

And he said, "Yeah if you really need me to," or "If you think it's necessary," or some extremely odd, condescending, incomprehensible thing.

I said, "YES, I DO."

But he kept getting distracted with his phone. He stayed on the bed and wasn't with me at all. I gave up trying to get him to help me keep track of my contractions. By now I was about to transition, and finally my friend/ savior showed up. My worthless husband left the room. It didn't take long for my friend to realize we needed to go!! I couldn't even make it to our car without stopping to breathe/scream through contractions. I must have been fully dilated on the ride to the hospital, just like in the movies. I was making a racket and cursing like a sailor over every bump, and my husband joked about not having the baby in the car. I remember looking over at him driving all calm and collected, and thinking, "What is going on in that thick beautiful skull?" I didn't know, I just knew I wanted to smash it in.

It was a very dramatic hospital entrance as I snarled at the front desk, "I DO NOT HAVE TIME FOR PAPERWORK." I have very few fond memories of my husband the second time. That's magnanimous. I have very few memories where, later, I didn't feel like kicking him in the balls. At the time I was very logical and none of these feelings surfaced.

The midwife checked me and said, "Wow you were trying to do this all by yourself, you're at 10cm." My mother-in-law was on her way and a nurse asked if we wanted to wait for her to show up. My husband responded, "She doesn't want to wait." That was my only memory where we were on the same page and he didn't let me down.

When I started pushing, the midwife told him to take my hand. It was like he was a wooden person, not my husband at all. It was the day my husband struck out, didn't show up to play, choked, failed, screwed me over, abandoned me, and betrayed me. I have had a hard time forgiving and letting go. I've raged at him and continue to sneak out snarky comments. Like the other day when he was suffering from the man flu. I brought him tea and dropped popcorn into his mouth because he felt like he was dying. He barely had the strength to open his mouth, let alone move his hands. We were giggling, and it was this cute silly moment. Then I said,

"I've given you more attention with the flu than you gave me during the birth of our second child."

And why oh why did it have to be true????? On Dec 14, 2016 I didn't have a choice but to be ALL IN. He had a choice. I didn't want to defame the man I love but the reason I'm telling this story is that I need to make sense of what my choices are and how I can find peace with them. **There are times when, we as women, literally don't have any option but to give it our all.** It is our body that gets taken over; our body that feeds a baby. If we don't show up, the baby suffers or dies.

Although my husband's lack of presence that day cast a shadow over our relationship for some time, I read back over my journals of the first year of baby number two and they are full of positive things about my husband and our life. I would come home from work to a super clean house and the delicious meals he cooked. He did many good things. But the truth is, even if my husband had showed up with his game face on December 14, even if he cleaned and cooked every day of his life with a smile on his face, I'm not sure he could make up for all I endured bearing and breastfeeding and loving his two children. But I think **I'm finally ready to stop** keeping track and just revel in my awesomeness — and his too. I will never stop noticing all the things that women do, and I will never stop trying to tip the balance.

So, beautiful women, thank you for showing up, for stepping up, for giving of your soft animal body, and sacrificing the many things you would have rather been doing when you were growing, bursting, nurturing life into existence. Then despite all that, you have another baby and start all over again. No one calls you "Superwoman." Your body took a toll, you soldier on, and you sacrifice. I am so proud you. I love you all.

THEY DIDN'T SEW
MY CERVIX SHUT

Something felt wrong. I went to the bathroom and knew something was wrong. They said that my cervix failed. I could feel him when I reached up inside of myself. When I went into the hospital, they didn't push him up; they didn't sew my cervix shut. The doctor who could perform a cerclage wasn't in on the weekend. By then my baby's sack had contracted a bacteria and my body decided he was no longer viable. He came out. He was in a little blue tub, still in his sack — but he was gone. They put him in a tiny little blanket that the Catholic Church gives, because they knew what was happening, but it was like a death box or a grief box — I don't know what to call it. He was getting enough oxygen to keep his heart beating for almost an hour, but it just wasn't enough. **After his heart stopped, he wrapped his hand around my finger; it was crazy.** I had an out-of-body experience. I was looking down at myself, my body was grieving but my mind was detached. I felt bad for a long time about not being present in my own body then — about having my son experience me crying instead of experiencing me loving him in those short moments. But he was there because he knew I needed him, or God knew, or the universe, or fate knew I needed him — or whatever you want to call it. My delivery nurse was there for me from the time he started coming out until four hours after he was born, and three hours after her shift had ended, she never left my side. **She streamed tears — the collar of her shirt was soaked.** I don't know how much it affected her, but the next week I brought her a rose to thank her. I don't know if she was there or not, but I left it for her.

STRIKE ONE, STRIKE TWO, STRIKE THREE

My entry into motherhood wasn't sunshine and daisies. From the moment I found out I was pregnant, I was scared. And I remained scared for 36 weeks and 6 days.

When I was diagnosed as a type 1 diabetic at 16, I swore off motherhood and proudly, loudly announced that I would never have a baby. I was terrified by everything I had heard about high-risk pregnancies and deemed I wasn't strong enough. After lots of discussion with my husband and doctors, we decided it wasn't as traumatizing as I had heard it can be.

Even though my pregnancy wasn't the shit show I had heard about on *The Maury Povich Show* when I was a teenager, it was far from a glowing, comforting time in my life. There was not a time during my pregnancy where I felt like my body knew what it was doing. I was constantly stressed, concerned and scared about having a baby with no limbs (thanks, Maury). The very beginning of a global pandemic was also a very interesting time to have my first child.

There were lots of doctor's appointments, lots of concern about her growth and heart thickness, lots of issues with regulating my blood sugars and maintaining my diabetes, and lots of terrible bedside manner by my fetal/maternal specialist. I never felt like I was the safest place for my daughter, but being told my womb had become toxic and we needed to be medically induced was a blow I wasn't ready to hear: Strike one. I had tried to do everything according to my doctors, but my body was rebelling and no longer cooperating.

Strike two came thirteen hours after my induction began. It was a long, slow, painful day of contractions. My OB proudly announced I had made it to 3cm during a cervical check, but then kept digging. **And digging. And digging.** Then the nurse was by my side, holding and rubbing my hand. Next, the portable ultrasound machine came in, but my doctor was hovering over my ribcage. Even though my daughter had been in the perfect position thirteen hours earlier, now "Everything has changed. If your water breaks, it will be fatal. We're going to the OR now."

I'll never forget the pain of being wheeled past a delivery room and hearing a mom successfully birth her child — as I was told I couldn't do the same. We got a few short minutes together as a happy family of three before she was whisked away to the NICU for "critically low blood sugar." **I was struggling with the drugs and aftermath of a C-section,** so I needed to stay in recovery while my husband went with our daughter. The second I could no longer see her, I started vomiting and didn't stop for eighteen hours until I could hold her again.

There were concerns over her blood and weight. She needed a feeding tube and bili lights, which meant I couldn't hold her. This led us to not being able to connect and breastfeed. **Strike three.**

Today, over two years later, she is the happiest, sassiest, most beautiful human being on the planet, and I am so proud to be her mom. We've both grown so much since she entered our realm, and I can't get enough of her. But, the idea of putting my body through everything again gives me severe anxiety. People say I'll change my mind, but I know deep down that **I cannot survive another pregnancy.** It's not just the pregnancy, either. I'm still working through PPA and trying to remember who I used to be prior to becoming a mom. I lost so much of myself during my pregnancy due to fear and stress.

Plus, my body can only make so much cute and our daughter emptied the reserves!

"There is no bigger agony than

an untold story inside you."

— Maya Angelou

——— • ———

SOMETHING'S COMING OUT, AND WE DON'T KNOW WHAT IT IS!

I was lucky to have my sister, ten years younger than me, living in town when I was pregnant. She came to all the birth classes with me, was there for my daughter's first kick (which scared the shit out of me — I screamed), and came to the hospital when it was time. I was in labor for eighteen hours before we decided to try Pitocin, and then the real show began. I was at 3cm one minute, and the next thing I knew, squishy things were coming out. My sister ran into the hall yelling, "Something's coming out, and we don't know what it is!" Turned out to be a twisted little part of the water sac.

Just as fast, the baby was crowning. I couldn't see it at the time, but my sister told me that she looked at the baby's head in horror thinking my child was misshapen. She looked at the doctor's and nurse's faces for a reaction that never came. She didn't know that a baby's skull overlaps in the birth canal. Thankfully, my little one's head smoothed right out, and we share the best birth memories.

MOANING LIKE AN ANIMAL AND PANTING IN HYPERVENTILATION

I didn't take time to process my resentments about giving birth to my second child for several months after the baby was born. I asked my husband **"What was going on with you? Why couldn't you put down your phone? Why did you act like you didn't care?"**

He stated three reasons:

1. *I was distracted because I was mad at your mom because she disappeared into her room with a headache just when you were going into labor.* (True story but even more of a reason for him to step up.)

2. *I thought it was going to be another thirty-hour labor and I was pacing myself.* (DID I LOOK LIKE I WAS PACING MYSELF WHEN I WAS MOANING LIKE AN ANIMAL AND PANTING IN HYPERVENTILATION?)

3. *I think something is wrong with me and I can only feel joy and excitement when something is novel.* (Yes closer to the truth; there was something wrong with you.)

WE KNEW PRENATALLY THAT MY DAUGHTER HAD DOWN SYNDROME

The labor of my second daughter came on fast, and on our way into Boston, I almost gave birth to her on the Mass Pike. We made it to the hospital, and she was born within two hours, after just one push. My husband and I immediately burst into tears upon hearing her fierce cry and seeing her strong movements. We knew prenatally that my daughter had Down syndrome and a serious heart condition. The entire room of nursing staff and doctors also began to cry. Everyone was moved to tears of joy that she arrived with such **strength** and **magic.** To this day, she brings that same strength and magic anywhere she goes.

YOU DO NOT CARE

Everyone always asks if women really poop during birth. Yes, you absolutely do. And no, you absolutely do not care.

YOU CAN SEE HIM WHEN YOU CAN WALK AROUND THE NURSES STATION

33 weeks. My husband got clearance for one last business trip, so he got on a plane. I was mid-trial. I got a call from my doctor's office: "Get a ride to the hospital or we are sending an ambulance. There is a problem with your labs." HELLP with none of the outward symptoms. My liver wasn't functioning. My kidneys weren't functioning. I couldn't clot blood. No platelets. Blood pressure totally fine. Looked fine on the outside. Very much dying on the inside. Emergency induction. C-section would cause me to bleed out. Epidural too risky. No drugs. A monsoon. My husband out of touch over the Pacific. Pitocin. His best friend from childhood. My work colleague. A nurse trained in birth hypnosis. A midwife who lied and said I could have meds if I just did a few test pushes. 4.7lbs. Eventually. Eventually. He cried. I got to touch him and then NICU. I got sicker. The preeclampsia finally came. So much magnesium I woke up unable to breathe. My husband arrived? A blood transfusion and a challenge: "You can see him when you can walk around the nurses' station without passing out." Determination. And with both of us hooked up to machines, a very overdue meeting. Of course, we are fine now. Practically inseparable. All he knows was that it was a dark and stormy night. I am extremely proud of us, grateful for good maternal medical care, and so so deeply traumatized

I HAD NEVER FELT SO MUCH LOVE AS WHEN SHE WAS PLACED IN MY ARMS

I spent my pregnancy worrying about what it would be like when I finally went into labor. I had heard so many stories about painful births from friends. The drive up the Alcan Highway at 8 ½ months pregnant, with all the bumps along the way, may have triggered my labor. She arrived two weeks earlier than expected, just after we arrived in Alaska. When my labor started, I remember thinking, "Wait a minute, this can't be it; I'm not feeling pain. This is easy. Fun even?" She was born in a rush, and I had never felt so much love as when she was placed in my arms. I held her tiny feet in my hands and recognized them from the way they felt when they pushed against my ribs when she was growing.

Twelve years later, looking back, I don't think I should have been worried about birth when I started the journey of motherhood. The journey after the birthing day is when things get difficult. How do I take care of my baby, work at the same time, and excel at both? How do I help my tiny daughter grow from a young lady into a responsible being who is happy, well-rounded, and well provided for? We have had our challenges: the time she jumped off her bed and cut a deep hole into her foot from a bad landing, when she was a toddler and fell off a dock in Kodiak and I pulled her up from the water, and when I found myself a single mom struggling to provide for us. Today, she is smack in the middle of pre-puberty, and I see that there are new challenges to navigate as a mom. When things get difficult, it always somehow turns out ok and I try not to worry.

A message for future mamas worrying about the birthing-day: It's a long journey. The birthing-day is just the start.

FROM WITHIN

"I'm very lucky to be pregnant,

but this is some bullshit."

— Amy Schumer

———— • ————

"GET IT ALL OUT" KIND OF VOMITING

Right around the time when I was figuring out that I was pregnant, I vomited in a trash can at Save-U-More. It was in the front entrance, right by the gumball machine, in front of the checkers, shoppers, God, and everybody. I'm certain it was loud and ugly, you know, that deep "get it all out" kind of vomiting. It came on so fast I had no time to make it anywhere else and believe me, I was as surprised as everyone watching. When I finished puking my guts out I stared into that can, for a good ten seconds; half wondering who was staring at me, and half deciding whether or not I could run to my car and immediately move out of Homer.

Eventually, I decided all I could do was wipe my mouth and apologetically stroll back to the produce section and own it. Was I embarrassed? Yes. Did I care? Mmm, I'm not sure. I was too concerned with my legitimate, **insatiable craving for red bell peppers and that horrible instant lemonade.** Little did I know, this is exactly what parenting would be like every single day. It's weird and messy and ridiculously embarrassing (especially in grocery stores). You can control almost nothing about what is happening except for your own attitude. And for some delusional reason, you always feel like you should be apologizing to someone about how you're doing it. You keep your head high and learn to not give a damn if anyone judges the vomit on your shirt (which by this point most likely isn't yours) and stay strong for that beautiful, wild, little creature you call "baby."

THINGS I DIDN'T KNOW ABOUT PREGNANCY

When you're pregnant, even your vulva gets fat.

After you have baby, they still rule your body: breastfeeding,
diet, backaches, no sleep.

Nine days of constipation post birth can be worse than the labor itself.

There is no break between giving birth and mothering.

We start on an empty tank and run on fumes for six months.

Your second pregnancy will be nothing like your
first pregnancy, so truly,

lap that shit up the first time 'round.

NO MATTER THE GENDER OF MY CHILD

Everything is still so fresh and new with my 10-week-old son. Before he was born, I didn't understand the concept of loving someone more every day and REALLY feeling it every day. Before he was born I was a little bummed I wasn't going to have a girl. I have a sister and mother who I'm really close with, and I wanted that kind of relationship with a daughter of my own. I wanted to teach her how to be a strong, compassionate, open-minded girl, and then woman. I wanted to show her that she can be independent, should stick up for herself and others, and can dream big — even if it might be hard work making that dream a reality. But now, having my son, I can't imagine it any other way. I wake up excited to see him (even though I just saw him a few hours before), and I absolutely love him more every day. I realize that no matter the gender of my child, I can instill in them to respect and empower women — and to be a strong, open-minded person. I look forward to what our relationship will grow into, and to see the person that he is going to become.

BABY ABSORBING BABY

We had tried just about everything to get pregnant. Medications, IUI, IUI with ultrasounds, etc. We finally decided to do IVF as a last resort. With IVF, we had one shot; it was too expensive to do twice. After all the shots and egg retrievals, we had three viable eggs. So, putting all of our eggs in one basket, as the saying goes, we implanted all three.

I was 40 years old, so we knew there was a chance of having multiples, but we also knew that the three implanted eggs increased our odds of conceiving at least one. Three weeks later we got the call, pregnant! Six weeks later at the first ultrasound, it was twins!! "Oh crap, I'm 40," I thought, "I'm not sure I'm equipped for two babies at the same time."

Eight weeks later, at peace with the idea of twins at a routine ultrasound appointment, the tech showed us the first baby. The wand moved, looking for the second heartbeat. Looking, looking, looking. Nothing.

The other twin stopped growing around 9 weeks, and unlike a miscarriage, my body and my daughter just absorbed it over the rest of the pregnancy. It was weird to grieve the loss of a baby while still pregnant with it's twin sister. Some days I look at my daughter and wonder if she absorbed the personality of both babies.

"Whatever happens to you belongs to you.

Make it yours. Feed it to yourself even if it feels

impossible… Let it nurture you,

because it will."

— CHERYL STRAYED

——— • ———

ONE, TWO, THREE, FOUR, FIVE

Driving through Utah on our way to Zion National Park, I keep checking my phone, looking for some bars. I can't believe our fate is dependent upon these wavering towers. We have an appointment with Dr. Soules, our new fertility doctor in Seattle. He will share the results from our latest testing. We have been told that we may not be able to have children, and I fear this is what he, too, will share.

Finally, we find some bars outside of the visitor's center in Bryce Canyon. I sit on hold. As I wait for our fate to be determined, I think about our fertility journey so far. One, two, three, four, five. **Five miscarriages.** Three years of scared elation and then heartache. Guilt and questions creep in, I have had two abortions, both with their own hard stories, but I still wonder if I deserve this. Am I too old at 37?

The list runs through my mind: Progesterone, Clomid, Saline Histogram, Estrogen, Femera, HCG trigger shots, D&C, surgery for my heart-shaped uterus, genetic testing, sperm tests, hormone tests, and more tests. Diagnosis: RPL (Recurrent Pregnancy Loss) with no known reason.

"You might want to stop doing this to yourself and your body," my doctor told me.

"It could be impossible with you and your husband's genetics," another doctor said.

I am traumatized. I am tired, tired of ovulation sex, tired of the grief and the disappointment, tired of losing my babies.

I quickly snap back to reality when Dr. Soules comes on the line. He says there is nothing wrong with us, with me, and we should continue trying. He sounds confident and tells us that there is no reason that we can't have a baby. He tells me I do have RPL. He says many women with this diagnosis are able to conceive with the TLC protocol, Tender Loving Care. I hang up the phone and cry. Cry with possibility and with hope.

Over dinner that night, my husband and I decide we will have no more interventions. As we drive across the country, our van rocks and rolls in rest stops and parking lots and everywhere in between. Arriving at our destination, my family home in New Hampshire, our pregnancy test has two pink lines.

For the entire pregnancy, we do the TLC protocol. Our son arrives safely. He is amazing.

Two years later, we decide to try for another child. I have another miscarriage. Again, we try. Again, pregnant. Again, scared.

Three months into the pregnancy, I am on a rare date with my husband. I feel something between my legs, use the restroom, look down and see a considerable amount of blood on my underwear. My heart drops, I feel sick. I think about a previous miscarriage I had at a concert. Same scenario, lots of people around, same sinking feeling. I walk to my husband and he drives me to the hospital. It's late and there is no one there to give me an ultrasound.

I am sobbing; I feel like I might die from another loss. They see and understand my trauma and call in an ultrasound tech.

By now, I know many of the techs. They have all seen me collapse into myself with pain that has nowhere to go. Some pray for me, one gives me an angel amulet, one barely looks or talks to me as I beg her to tell me what is wrong. Fortunately, on this particular night, the tech that walks in is the tech I had for my last miscarriage. She was kind and honest about what she was seeing. This time, she sees me crying and gives me a loving smile. She turns on the ultrasound machine and guides me through everything. There on the monitor appears my son, heart beating. My whole body lets out a sob of relief. Everyone gathers around me, and the tech hugs me tightly as I cry in relief.

Six months later, he is on my chest, searching for me with his beautiful blue eyes. I am so in love. As I think back on our journey and I look at these two incredible humans that we have created, I am in complete awe. It truly is a miracle to have a child.

THEY TOOK HER BABY

"You're getting fat. What are you pregnant?" she said matter-of-factly, on the other side of the desk at the shelter office. I smiled, having known this moment was coming. She sat looking at me, her belly rounded. "Yes," I said.

We did the math and realized that our babies would be born weeks apart.

I think we were talking about finding housing or maybe about the need for her to be kind to the other women in the shelter. Her words were frequently loud and hard, sharpened by years of poverty, neglect, and bruises. We were about the same age. All of her kids were in foster care or adopted. I was pregnant with my first baby. It was easy to find reasons not to like her. She shouted at the other women in the shelter, making them feel scared. She hid bologna in her dresser that made the shared room smell. Her survival skills were well-honed and did not endear her to others.

But I liked her anyway. She was delighted by the news that we were both pregnant. She enjoyed knowing more than me about pregnancy and what it took to become a mom. For once, she could tell me how to live my life instead of the other way around. She knew those hard first weeks after birth. She understood the changes happening in my life in ways I could not.

While the news of my first child was met with excitement and smiles by family and friends, the news of her baby brought consternation and fear. There was doubt whether she would even be allowed to bring her baby home from the hospital. While the pregnancy had made her feel hopeful — another chance at getting things right — it also made her angry. What right did "those people" have to take her baby? What would happen?

I wanted so many things for her. I wanted to undo all the injustice and abuse from her childhood. I wanted to find her supportive housing where she would learn the skills of how to be a mother. I wanted her deep, unsatisfied needs to be met so she could meet the needs of this baby.

I went on maternity leave a month before my baby was born — before her baby was due to be born too. In the whirlwind of last-minute preparations, I don't remember the last time I saw her. But I heard a version of what happened. She brought the baby home! But one day, when the few-week-old baby wouldn't stop screaming in the grocery store, she screamed back at her wailing infant. She was reported. The baby was taken away.

I also had a baby that wouldn't stop crying for many days and nights. And every time we were in the car, my baby would cry the entire drive— whether it was fifteen minutes or four hours. Sometimes I wanted to shout. Sometimes I did. Sometimes I lay her wailing body in the crib and would go on the porch and feel sick and cry. I didn't know how to do this. I had a stable life but still couldn't pull it together. My husband left for work early and came home late most days. I was alone, more than I had expected. And the baby kept crying. Often wouldn't nap. Everyone told me I was a good mom and not to be so hard on myself. I thought of my shelter friend, and how everyone seemed to root for my family to succeed, whereas everyone had been waiting, expecting her to fail.

I thought I knew better than her, but really, what did I know?

IMPENDING VOMIT

Morning Sickness: a cutesy, sweet, non-threatening, non-medical sounding term. Clearly invented by men. For me, the so-called **morning sickness** was an all-day, all-night, cloying, screaming nausea, for twenty-two weeks. Acid raging up my throat, sweaty and shaky with impending vomit all day. Waking up at night, trying to decide if I was actually going to throw up, debating whether I'd get more rest by sleeping on the bathroom floor. Every food, drink, and smell made me sick. Flowers made me sick. The sight of food emojis made me hurl. And somehow... I was expected to function. Showering, getting dressed, crying, laying down, before driving to work. Pregnant women should be pampered at spas and venerated at award ceremonies!

That was **hard**. I was **strong**.

"Remember our heritage is our power;

we can know ourselves and our capacities by

seeing that other women have been strong."

— JUDY CHICAGO

——— • ———

YOU NEVER REALLY GET RID OF THAT MUSCLE MEMORY

I don't usually talk about my pregnancy, birthing story, or the first two years of my son's life. I stick to more upbeat topics.

I was nearly 6 months pregnant. On a routine checkup, the midwives noticed my stomach wasn't protruding at the rate it should be. I wasn't gaining weight, and neither was my baby. At first, I didn't worry because they told me there was nothing to worry about. However, they put me on weekly check-ups to monitor the situation. Two weeks later, they were beginning to worry because the lack of growth had continued and was becoming exponentially alarming. They told me I needed twice-weekly ultrasounds to monitor the baby's growth and vital signs. I was further reassured that all was well, and I dutifully continued to work full time, despite increasing pain and discomfort.

At 6 ½ months, I finished with my (at this point, routine) ultrasound check-up and headed to work. I'd barely left the hospital when I received an emergency call. **They were immediately putting me on a plane to send me to a specialist.** My baby's life depended on it. That was the end of any chance for an idyllic, worry-free pregnancy.

I flew out of Homer on the next commercial flight to Anchorage and went straight to the front of the line at the specialist's office. She told me there was indeed something very wrong that was keeping my baby from developing at a normal rate and put me on bed rest for the remainder of my pregnancy. I must try to keep my child alive and growing inside of my belly for another month to ensure he would survive birth, she explained. She would induce me at 8 months gestation IF he was still alive… because that would be the point where his viability odds would increase in the outside world versus staying in my belly. She made sure I understood she'd see me in one month IF he was still viable. She sent me home in shock and disbelief to process everything from my bed.

I had to quit my job immediately that afternoon. Timing being what it was, my baby shower was scheduled for that weekend. I didn't know what to tell anyone. My baby might not make it? Was I understanding that correctly? I was afraid to say anything. No one beyond my closest circle knew my anguished news. At the shower, I tried to fake happiness, but really I just wanted to cry. I was the only one who wasn't celebrating, and it felt awful to hold the gifts and not know if my son would ever use them.

It only took a week and one more concerning ultrasound appointment for the midwives to stick me back on a plane to Anchorage, where the specialist determined I must spend the remainder of my pregnancy admitted to Providence Children's Hospital's Maternity Ward on continuous monitoring. I was not allowed to walk. I had to ask permission to use the bathroom, and they would wheel me the equivalent of 15 steps in a wheelchair. They fed me double meals and explained how every calorie possible must go to my baby. I lost my autonomy completely, and slowly my self-respect faded away. I felt like a prisoner. Like I was seen as nothing more than an incubator for my son. Of course, I understood the seriousness and wanted the best for my baby, so I put my own needs on the back burner and laid there motionless for the month, until the morning they induced me.

My son didn't want to come out. He instinctively knew it was too early to be birthed and refused to budge. I was in labor for 3 ½ days. Yes, 3 ½ days. They were an hour from taking me to the table for a C-section when he finally decided to cooperate. It's all a horrible blur — from 6:00 am Tuesday until Friday at 9:52 pm, when he made his entrance.

Days of agony and detachment from my body.

No food allowed. No sleep, though I passed out more than once because of unbearable pain. I pulled every single muscle and wore my body out completely, even muscles I did not know I had. It took two weeks post-birth for me to walk without pain. I can't even begin to describe the discomfort using the bathroom. I would scream in agony for the first several days, after which I could keep the scream muffled, despite the pain persisting for weeks. You never really get rid of that muscle memory.

No part of this was natural. It was invasive torture, but I was told it was necessary to keep my son alive. He was born at 4lbs 13 oz (it had all been worth it — he had doubled in size in the final weeks at Providence). But by the following day, he had dropped to 4lbs 4 oz and was beginning to show signs of destabilization. They put him on a strict feeding schedule, and though I'd not slept in days, I found a new level of Superwoman within me as I found the energy to care for my son above all else.

It took five days to stabilize him to a point where they let me take him home. They put him on a high-calorie supplement to help him gain weight, and every day became structured around feeding and weighing him. He was tiny. I could hold him in one hand, yet he required 2000 calories a day minimum to keep him from wasting away.

Due to further complications, he was airlifted back to Providence when he was 6 weeks old. Blood transfusions, ICU stays, living in and out of hospitals for the first two years. I was repeatedly told it was a miracle he was still alive. Me sacrificing everything I had to help my son. I did nothing for three straight years except give my baby anything and everything he needed to keep him alive.

It took three or four years for him to stabilize enough that the doctors decided he might live after all. Slowly, people came back around... after the worst of it was over. After he was stabilized. After I could hide the trauma enough to pretend all was okay. Then people began to talk to me again. After it became apparent he was finally healthy, my family began to welcome us — like I could just forget the years of silence?

I lost everything I used to call my life. I lost my friends. I even lost my family. **It turns out there are only a few people in the world who can handle being around a mother faced with the grief of a dying child.** But I gained a whole new perspective, a whole new world, and a fiercely unshakable group of people from unexpected backgrounds who somehow understood where I was broken and believed in me.

Nobody talks about these aspects — the sacrifices we make as mothers to bring another life into the world. We are chosen as their incubators, and must do what is required of us. We have no choice to opt-out.

We are taught to believe the birth of a child should be one of the most joyous points in our lives. We put it on a pedestal and challenge every woman to attain the pinnacle of perfection, lest she be judged as inadequate or a complete failure as a mother. I feel that societal shame when I say out loud that it was one of the most traumatic and horrible chapters of my life.

And, how can I honor my trauma, yet ALSO honor my son and explain to him that his birth was indeed the most beautiful, love-filling, expansive, life-changing, best thing that ever happened to me? **The deep trauma is forever deeply entangled with exquisite perfection** — sometimes it's too hard to decipher. So I just let it be.

AVOID BEARING CHILDREN AT ALL COSTS

On July 4th, 2022, my husband and I celebrated our 25th wedding anniversary. Twenty-five years ago, I was focused on finishing up a work project, getting a run in before the ceremony, and hoping my sweat glands would not betray me at the courthouse. Having children and starting a family was the farthest thing from my mind that day. I had no idea that I had contracted a virus as a teenager, which, in turn, had affected my kidneys. I had no idea that getting pregnant should not have been in my cards. Had doctors known what was lurking in my body, they would have told me to avoid bearing children at all costs. I had no idea that my kidneys would be the root of HELLP in my first pregnancy and preeclampsia in my second, nor that twenty years down the road, I would end up on dialysis, my kidneys so scarred by it all that they were failing. Finally, when I ran through the park that day, I had no idea that I would not be spending my silver anniversary strolling a beach with my husband; instead, he would be on an operating table, one of his kidneys taken out to help me survive. On our wedding day, I had no idea, as most young women do not, what bearing children and having a family truly means. I had absolutely no idea whatsoever about anything I was saying "yes" to twenty-five years ago. But, I know now, without a doubt, I would say "Yes" to all of it, all over again.

IT WAS RADICAL. IT WAS
EMOTIONAL. IT WAS MAGIC.

When I became pregnant with my second, my first-born was 14 months old. I had weaned her the week before I saw the pink lines appear on the stick. We wanted another baby eventually, but were in a short-term summer rental and needed to move in six weeks. We had moved so many times, and looked for a home for nearly three years. I wanted my home before becoming pregnant again. I wanted to have a baby's room — that wasn't a crib in a lofted cabin. I wanted my first born to be potty-trained, and able to keep her boots on for the sake of keeping her feet dry. But here we were, about to have two under two while still renting.

My plan was to just keep up with the toddler — as if I had a choice. This meant my water intake was much less than the first time around and my prenatal vitamin regimen was totally relaxed. There were no regular prenatal massages or acupuncture for my lower back pain. I was too exhausted for lap swim after chasing the toddler around. I had complete trust my body was doing what it needed for baby number two, but I did not feel connected with this baby like I had the first.

We ended up falling into a beautiful home to rent through the winter (a home we would later come to buy, thankfully). One evening after the toddler was in bed I opted to take a bath and began meditating about the upcoming arrival of baby. I distinctly remember soaking with my big belly, wondering if this would be the last time in my life I would be pregnant. I pushed around the soft spots of my 34-week belly until I found the rump and then I sunk down below the surface of the water until my ears slowly filled with the warm water. My eyes rolled back and lids closed as I sunk further until only my nose and mouth were above the surface. My hands on my baby, through my belly. I listened to my own heartbeat... and in that moment realized my heartbeat was exactly what baby was hearing at that moment. It was radical. It was emotional. It was magic, for the first time in the pregnancy. Here we were listening together, and no one else would hear it like we were at that moment. I floated and synthesized with this new, completely unique little life.

FIVE PREGNANCIES: ONE ABORTION, TWO MISCARRIAGES, AND TWO LIVE BIRTHS

I've had five pregnancies: one abortion, two miscarriages, and two live births. All different experiences. I was a different person for each one and after each one. At 25, I was in the throes of alcoholism and drug use. I was homeless and trying to get on my feet. I found out I was pregnant when I was finishing my first trimester. I was such a wild child that missing my period didn't occur to me. I took a test and cried. And drank. I had fleeting romanticized thoughts about keeping the baby — but there was no way in hell that I was remotely ready. I was in my second trimester when I had my abortion. They didn't tell me what the hormone drop would do to me. I **basically went through postpartum depression.** I was a mess. I mean, I was a mess regardless, but I was a super mess afterward.

Seven years later, in a completely different state with a different fella — I was ten days late. There's no fuckin' way I was pregnant. I **had a an IUD in,** good for ten years, and I was on year four! When that positive came back — I cried, y'all. I was not ready to stop partying! I know it sounds shallow, but drugs and alcohol reigned supreme. And I already bought the mushrooms I was going to do that weekend.

But I knew I was ready. I was with a partner who wanted the same things. We wanted to start a family but were hoping to wait a couple of years. Oh well. My second pregnancy was the longest time since I started drinking, that I was 100% sober.

After my kid was born, I continued to drink. But not even an inch of what

I used to, and I stopped doing the other drugs I used to dabble with. Two years after my kid was born, I decided I was done after half a drink one night. It didn't serve me anymore. I didn't like who I was when I drank — not ten-drink me, not even half-drink me. Not a good look, let me tell you. Very chaotic — would I cry? Would I punch someone? Would I try to make out with everyone? Would I look for crack? That bitch was too much. She wasn't fun anymore, and I had a kid…**a kid who will forever and ever be more fun and outrageous than any shot of whiskey or one-night stand.**

What they don't tell you about sobriety is that — it fucking sucks. All the coping mechanisms you had are out the window. You are not only raw dogging reality, but you're also staring straight into all the bullshit that caused you to drink in the first place, and all the trauma that kept that blackout train choo choo chooin! Insert therapy here. Insert a million "aha" and "oh fuck" moments. Insert self-reflection and self-learning. Insert trying for baby number two, and insert my first miscarriage.

It was one of the super fun missed miscarriages. The kind where you walk around all, "Yay I'm pregnant and feel awful, and this is so great!!!" while the baby inside has stopped growing. My body knows I already have trust issues, why did she have to do me this way?!

I was 11 weeks when I found out the baby stopped growing at 8 weeks. Let's just say ugly crying in a paper mask with the ultrasound tech is not ideal.

So I had three options — and I chose to take Misoprostol and pass the fetal tissue at home. It took forever. The plan was to take the meds and pass it before my kid got home. It started right when my kid walked through the door. Awful cramps set, and the rest is the rest. That was hard, y'all. That was hard to bounce back from.

We tried again that December. And seven weeks later, I got out of my car to pick my kid up from daycare, when I felt a huge gush of fluid. I knew what was happening. I put my kid in the car, called my doctor, and was told how sorry she was, and, "There's nothing we can do. Call if your pad fills up super fast." I went through this one alone. **My husband was out of town. It was just me and my kid and my tears.** You start to feel silly for even getting excited. Like you just made a fool of yourself. Why did I even tell one person I was pregnant?! I didn't want to try again. I just wanted to give up. Things had shifted. I felt numb. What was wrong with me? Was it me? Was it my husband? Is the universe trying to tell me I'm a shit mom and stop procreating?

We went camping that fall, and I ate a turkey sandwich. All of a sudden, it seemed vomit worthy to me. I couldn't eat it anymore. When we got home I took a pregnancy test and — anxiety slapped me in the face — **you're positive bitch**. Pregnancy is a hell of a lot scarier when you try for it, really want it, and have had some losses under your belt. But this baby persevered. I went to some dark places during my pregnancy — some really awful scenarios played in my head. I said affirmations daily to ease the consistent uncertainty. It wasn't until I felt the baby kick that my anxiety eased up, and I got to enjoy my pregnancy — even the really awful parts. My baby was born healthy and happy (and with one of the most beautiful umbilical cords I have ever seen — I mean it was THICK and spiraling — oof! — tooting my own horn here). My beautiful, perfect older kid has a beautiful, perfect sibling. I'm a 100% sober mom. I've had five pregnancies; each one I had a choice. Would I do it all over again? Yes — a hundred million times — yes.

DEEPER PLACES

"I have not lost my power because I have been making sandwiches for a kid instead of playing the piano. I have not lost my power because I have been cleaning dishes and picking up legos and reading *What The Ladybird Heard* for the 45th time instead of playing the piano. I have not lost my power because I have spent one hundred hours on the phone with other mothers, trying to make sense of a shuddering planet.

I have not lost my power. I have found my power in the crushed cheerios, in the stinking vomit-covered over-alls that I have washed by the side of the road using a bottle of water. I have found my power in the dark and fierce shine of my child's eyes when he tells me, as he is falling asleep, that he is working on telling his nightmares what to do.

When I have time and am ready, I am going to make a noise so inflammatory, so holy, so broken, so deafening, so honest, and so absolutely goddamned powered that you will question what music even means."

— AMANDA PALMER

WE'RE MADE FOR THIS SHIT.

"I hate to tell you this girl, but we're made for this shit." That's what my sister-in-law told me.

Three months post-baby, I was feeling depleted: physically, emotionally, and spiritually. I felt like a warm moving corpse with only space between my ears and very sore nipples. I couldn't even escape to Netflix without feeling inept because I couldn't follow any plot unless I was both hearing English and reading English via closed captions. Even then, I still had to re-watch all the time.

Hearing that "we're made for this" was both affirming and totally devastating. It's a complicated feeling when you feel both incompetent as a human in the world, and also like a ruthless maternal machine capable of doing anything it takes — for as long as it takes — to keep her baby sleeping.

I had to bounce for hours on my yoga ball. It was my baby's cure-all and my nemesis: our drug. I guess I was made for it because I just kept bouncing. All morning. All afternoon. All evening, bounce bounce bounce. My husband couldn't bounce for longer than a few minutes...because it wasn't comfortable for his back, he told me. At that moment I realized he hadn't automatically sacrificed his own comfort the moment she was born like I had. Huh.

MOMMM! YOU ARE BEAUTIFUL!

I gained a lot of weight during my late thirties pregnancies. I nursed two babies for a combination of fifty-one months. Both left my body with maps of stretch marks, wider hips and sagging boobs. Did I mention the leg veins? Oh, the leg veins.

Feeling particularly down about these changes after a shower, I sulked naked across our family room to grab my clothes out of the bedroom. On seeing me, my 3-year-old's eyes lit up, and he exclaimed, "MOMMM! You are beautiful!" His reaction was unprompted and pure. It landed right in my center, softening and shifting how I see my new body. I earned every mark, sag, vein and bulge creating and giving life — how could that be anything other than beautiful?

MY BODY SEEMS FOREIGN BUT BABY IS HEALTHY

After a surprise pregnancy and nine months of getting used to the idea of my new role, I outlined my birth "preferences." I always wanted an unmedicated home or water birth, but for some reason, I felt the need to be at a bigger hospital. Being an intensive care nurse during Covid made me more anxious about all the things that could go wrong. I hoped to go into labor naturally, but was induced early due to low amniotic fluid. The medication they gave me to start labor is also used for medication-induced abortions. It doesn't make sense that some deem medication is only appropriate when it's for birth.

Contractions started, but I was barely dilated. Because I wasn't progressing, the interventions increased: balloon catheter, Pitocin, forced water breaking — which revealed meconium in my fluid. I had hoped to labor without pain medication. But **Pitocin is a synthetic oxytocin, and it's one hell of a drug.** I was writhing and shaking in pain, my heart rate sky-rocketed, and I needed the epidural twenty-four hours after the initial induction. I am a redhead and require more anesthesia, and the epidural wore off, so I had to get another dose. This dropped my blood pressure, requiring vasopressors to keep my blood pressure up, and thus perfusion to the baby.

After forty hours of labor in a windowless room, I was prepped for a C-section. I was devastated. But the OB came in for test pushes and said we could go for it. I pushed for 4.5 hours, vomiting on myself for the majority of that time. As any laboring woman knows, you just don't care anymore at some point. I hated being forced to lie on my back with people holding my legs. I wanted to be on my knees, which felt better to me for pushing.

My catheter wasn't working because his head was occluding my bladder. **They had filled me with seven liters of fluid to try to cushion since they broke my fluid.** The pain in my bladder was excruciating. At the end, the OB came in and called the NICU to be present at birth. My partner said he would never forget the sound of her ripping my vagina open. The relief I felt as he came out was indescribable. The OB promised to put a catheter in after she stitched me up. I didn't know I had torn.

Baby boy was finally born nearly forty-five hours after I was induced. The OB threw him on me, and he was gray. I had only a few seconds of him on my chest before he was whisked away.

I was yelling at them, **"Is he ok?"**

No one answered.

I heard people yelling,"Staff assist!" and the room swarmed. They were calling out the seconds my baby wasn't breathing. Finally, I heard a cry. Someone said, **"83% on room air."** They put a mask on him. I yelled at my mom to take pictures. I was sobbing but couldn't move, couldn't sit up. The OB was trying to deliver my placenta. It was the wrong color and didn't look like a normal placenta. The NICU team took my partner and our baby away. Someone came and told me our baby was breathing, but they were taking him for work up, and he had a CPAP on. The NICU doctor came back and told me he had multiple pneumothorax (holes popped in his lungs) from taking his first breath. They made it seem ok.

Two hours later, the nurses took me to see him. My partner was holding his tiny hand. His other hand was bandaged with an IV. He had monitors and cords all over him. They were on telehealth with a Seattle Children's Hospital neurologist. The doctor said, "She's an ICU nurse; you can talk to her." They told me they didn't think they needed to cool him. My brain was racing. Cooling is only done in post-cardiac arrest patients.

She showed me a paper with his arterial blood gas numbers. I start hyperventilating and sobbing because those numbers aren't compatible with life. People try to calm me down and tell me babies are different, and he is self-correcting but still grunting when breathing.

He can't breastfeed yet.

He looks so helpless.

I can't calm down.

We haven't even named him yet. My partner is crying because he didn't realize how bad it was and neither did I. We are both in shock.

The staff leaves, and we look at each other and ask about his name. My partner says, "I like Merritt." I said, "I do too."

That evening, the doctor came to our room and showed me my son's blood gas numbers. She said to keep them because it was extraordinary how he had corrected them in six hours. She asked if I wanted to try to feed him. We went to his room every three hours, and I squeezed colostrum from my breasts and fed him with a dropper, determined to avoid donor milk or formula. He latched once he came to our room. We went home on a Monday. The fresh air made me feel like I had been inside a prison. I sobbed as I left the hospital.

Four weeks later, I went under general anesthesia to repair my perineal tear that had re-ruptured at some point, probably due to constipation. I had thought in those weeks postpartum that it was normal to have that much pain.

I'm now eleven weeks postpartum and I just got cleared for activity. My anxiety, depression, and post-trauma stress have been terrible. I finally talked to the OB about getting on medication for postpartum anxiety and depression. I started walking. My body seems foreign, but my baby is healthy. He smiles. He moves constantly. He is so alert and active and interested in the world around him. Everyone has a birth story. I just hadn't imagined mine would be like this. It has made me realize I'm stronger than I thought and to trust my gut. I guess there was a reason I wanted to deliver at a bigger hospital.

"There is no greater power

on this earth than story."

— LIBBA BRAY

——— • ———

I WRITE THIS NOT KNOWING WHAT THE FUTURE HOLDS

Pure exhaustion, beyond any flu; vulnerability that can't be tamed, tunnel vision, a certainty of my last breath and last heartbeat right here on the middle of my living room floor, my home where I feel so safe.

The fear that surrounded my every thought and every move after this moment has brought me here. Rewind nine months.

I wanted more than anything to have one more baby.

I felt like it would complete our family, that I would know that this is the last, and that my youngest (I have two girls) would make the best big sister.

My husband did not want another, was adamant, and it was devastating to me. However, his technique was not foolproof, and I half-guilty took that pregnancy test knowing the two lines about to appear would change everything.

He tried not to act excited, but something in him that day changed. He told his friends immediately, and I knew that Mr. Tough Guy wasn't as tough as he seemed.

The running joke on his lobster boat was that there was some type of contagion going on, as his sternman had just found out that his spouse was pregnant, and just a few weeks later, his third man announced the same. Three guys on a lobster boat, all with pregnant ladies. What are the odds?

There was lots of excitement as the holidays came along, and with my brother's wedding around the corner…and then STOP.

Cramps. Maybe I ate something? The intensity rises. Maybe I'll lay down?

In fear, Googling for answers, then I have to pee.

My water broke all over the floor… at 10 weeks.

The first words I uttered as I sat confined to the toilet were, "I lost my chance."

I would never question my husband's love for me after that night. Four hours of trying to lie down, then trying to make it to the toilet, with blood everywhere, and my husband cleaning on his hands and knees. He looked at me and said, **"Your lips are white. Either I take you in the truck, or I'm calling the ambulance."** His words sounded so far away. "Your truck," I said. About halfway to the hospital, I remember laying in the back seat feeling as though I wouldn't make it, that my heart was giving out. Nurses and doctors whisked me out of the truck and, within minutes, had me hooked up to an IV, taking samples. Ultrasound technician: "No baby." My doctor: "Emergency surgery."

My placenta wasn't detaching, and I had been bleeding out for hours. A nurse held my hand within minutes, saying, "I'll be right here. Sleep."

I woke up pain-free, joking with the nurses and grateful to be alive. Somewhere around 3:00 am, sadness set in. Grieving was hard. I found wonderful friends, while other people became strangers. Signs of hearts and rainbows surrounded me.

The ride home from the hospital was quiet. Then my husband said, "If you want to try again, I want to too."

Life slowly started again, and I knew in my heart I wanted to try again. Spring had come, and my 33rd birthday was around the corner. My husband and I planned to keep our next pregnancy quiet, just in case. We had announced the last pregnancy early and, therefore, had to tell the world when we miscarried.

Two pink lines made their grand appearance after my birthday, but this pregnancy took on an unfamiliar role with constant worry and anxiety. The genetic results of the last pregnancy had come back normal, so what went wrong? Was I too lax with what I put in my body? Did I exercise too much? What went wrong? I asked myself 1,000 times. I questioned *everything*. Each day felt like an accomplishment with no cramps and no bleeding. I had a countdown chart to 12 weeks, the ultimate "safe date" to share the news — even though I knew women who had miscarried beyond 12 weeks.

My pregnancy was not smooth; I threw my back out for the first time, tripped across the backyard and fell on my stomach, had migraines, and had shingles three times. It was during the Covid-19 pandemic, so add in homeschooling. Stress took over.

Then, just as I pictured it in my head, I wiped, and there was blood.

I told myself to lay down and rest, that it would be okay.

The next morning, my youngest daughter, who always snuggled up to me in the morning, woke me up.

"Mommy, you see the little girl?"

"Little girl?"

"Yes, Mommy, she's sitting on your bureau and she's smiling at us."

I tried to shake it off, but inside, I felt this was the first baby, who we had named Sophie, coming to take the other baby. This was the cynical side of me that had taken over with this pregnancy.

No more bleeding, so maybe Sophie was just saying hi.

Fast forward to the ultrasound appointment that I so anxiously awaited. My husband would only be able to Facetime due to Covid.

In my mind, I prepared myself for the worst.

And in perfect timing, like a bad dream, the ultrasound technician uttered the words, **"There's a gestational sac, there are the ovaries, there's the placenta … I'm going to be honest with you. There's no baby."**

I can bring myself back to the moment in an instant. No matter how much you prepare yourself, the tears still flood. My poor husband, home, helpless.

What should have been a joyous day where my husband had the kids, while I went to the local gardening shop to pick out a bush in honor of Sophie, turned into a Friday from hell.

First blood work, then an OB appointment. I went to the garden center to pick out two plants, took a Covid-19 test, and scheduled surgery for Monday.

The weekend was filled with dread of the impending surgery.

6:00 am Monday: I cried my way through saying goodbye to my daughters and husband, and like it shouldn't happen, he dropped me off at the hospital entrance alone. Some of my longest walks have been in hospitals, mostly memorizing the style of the floor through my tears.

Everything went as smoothly as it could go and I found myself saying, "It is what it is." I mean, what was I going to do about it?

The same nurse came in and promised she would hold my hand again, she was a Godsend.

Terrified, I held her hand and drifted to sleep.

When I awoke, I wanted to get back to my husband who was waiting in the parking lot. I was so nauseous. Off we went home. I quickly dove back into work and kept as busy as possible. I had a hundred stressors, and no one seemed to understand that I needed a break, not even myself. I kept hearing myself say, "I need a break," but like a lot of mommies, I also thought "This will pass and I will be ok," and I just continued on.

Two weeks later, **STOP.**

I felt pure exhaustion, beyond any flu, a vulnerability that can't be tamed, tunnel vision, a certainty of my last breath and last heartbeat right there on the middle of my living room floor, in my home where I usually feel safe.

That day was June 22, 2020. My first panic attack. My first sign of postpartum depression and anxiety.

A little over three weeks later, and I am still alive and survived what I thought was going to kill me. I've had multiple attacks and was put on Ativan (I hate medicine) to find a reprieve. I learned **hormones suddenly drop two weeks after a miscarriage.** Perhaps I had a chemical imbalance.

My OB fast tracked me to a psychiatrist who is helping me find the right fit to get me balanced again. My therapist answers my calls. I've had multiple ER visits and calls to the doctor. I hired a babysitter once a week, and moved myself and children in with my mother, who is home fairly consistently to help me. These are all the things that have helped me get to writing this.

Postpartum is talked about with moms who have babies, but it isn't spoken of much when it comes to miscarriage. It might be argued that with miscarriage, women go through all the hormonal changes more quickly, as they are not breastfeeding and their cycles come back much faster.

I write this not knowing what the future holds, but knowing that I'm doing my best to get through this. I want women to know that you are not alone and there are wonderful people out there to help. Listen to yourself, take breaks, and love yourself.

"I did not know that I was supposed to feel everything. I thought I was supposed to feel happy."

— GLENNON DOYLE

——— • ———

SELF-CARE

I was thinking the other day about how I am not doing any self-care lately, ever since the baby was born. It dawned on me — **if I don't practice my own self-care, how will my child learn to?** Isn't that funny, that I should be inspired to massage oil into my skin only after thinking of the impact it will have on my daughter?

THREE HOT MESSES

I remember one evening shortly after maternity leave and coming home from work/daycare with both girls. Zeliah was only about 4 months old — tired, hungry, and still figuring out breastfeeding. Gwen was barely 2, and probably didn't like her dinner that night. **They were both crying, and as I sat in my kitchen, half undressed trying to breastfeed, with one crying baby on my lap and another crying kid in her high chair, I felt so defeated, tired, and all I could do was sit there and cry with them.** At which point my husband arrived home to three hot messes to deal with. God bless him. It wasn't the only instance that all three of us ended up in tears together, but I'm glad to say we made it through those few tough months and life has certainly gotten easier!

THIS BABY FELT FOREIGN TO ME AND I COULDN'T TELL ANYONE

I know now that I experienced postpartum depression with both of my boys, but to different degrees. Back then, there really wasn't a word for it.

I prepared relentlessly for the birth of my first. I read every article, read tons of books, and listened to endless advice on how to raise a baby. My fear of Motherhood morphed into excitement. But I was unprepared for how I felt when I left the hospital.

My first son came into the world in the midst of family drama on my son's father's side, transforming something that should be beautiful into one of the most stressful times of my life. Back then, birthing wasn't like it is now. There were no water tubs, lowlights, or beautiful private rooms filled with serenity and peace. It was a regular room in which the nurse came in every hour, put your legs up in stirrups, measured your cervix with her fingers, and called the doctor only when it was time.

I had to drive myself to the hospital because my son's father had been drinking all night. My mother was the only person I wanted in the room. My baby was born with me watching my mother's eyes as he left my body. There was no comfort, no support except for my mom. He was whisked away to get checked. I spent the second night alone with my baby, as my son's father had to "rest up" for work. So, was I feeling postpartum depression, or was it just plain, regular depression? I would have leaned towards run-of-the-mill depression, except for the feelings that followed.

I arrived home the first day with my baby to a houseful of family. I was tired, unsure of what to do, and overwhelmed with everyone arguing about how

I was supposed to push up the bag inside the bottle to get the bubbles out. I felt alone from that moment on, and even when I wasn't, I still was.

I felt alone, and I felt … nothing. I would get up every night, every morning, every time feeding was approaching and just do it. I wasn't happy, sad, mad, or anything like that. I just did what I had to do. People complimented me on my patience and even keel with my baby. But that wasn't really what it was … I just kept keepin' on keepin' on.

The doctor visits were frequent due to all the wellness checks, vaccines, etc. I look back and realize that **not once did my son's doctor or my doctor ask me how I was feeling. I didn't offer any insight into my feelings, out of fear they would then know I didn't have the "nurturing nature" that all moms should.** If the doctor had asked, I likely wouldn't have been truthful, anyway. I did not want anyone to think I did not love my baby or think I was sad that my life had changed so quickly.

There were no negative feelings, no positive ones either. Over the following months, it felt like I was playing a part in a movie, acting and reciting the script of Motherhood, as it was supposed to be. I would watch everyone exclaiming over this cute, happy baby and would dig really deep to reflect the same excitement back. I was never angry, like I hear happens so often. I was just going through the motions.

Some days my son would giggle, and my heart would leap. Other days, he would giggle, and I would tickle his belly and move on. I fed him, changed him, cooed and played with him, all the right things, all the required things. But I wasn't overwhelmed with joy and love. This baby felt foreign to me, and I couldn't tell anyone because then I would be a Bad Mother. I mean, "real" Mothers, Good Mothers, love their babies the moment they are placed on their chest, right? I didn't feel that at all, and to this day I avoid the eyes of anyone that says this.

My postpartum depression did not end suddenly. In fact, I am not even sure how I beat this thing I didn't know I had. I slowly started relishing in my son's milestones and antics. I would see him crawl and be filled with pride, a real feeling! My giggles with him over silly things became genuine, and every day became a new adventure that I looked forward to instead of dreading. One day, I found myself sobbing over his sweet, little sleeping body. It was not because I thought I didn't love him or that I thought I was a bad mom; it was because my heart was bursting with love for this sweet little boy that now owned my heart. When I focus on the relationship I have forged with him today, I know I am a really good mom. I have put those dark days in the background of my heart.

My second baby was different. My postpartum depression was nowhere near the degree that I experienced with my firstborn. My worries before his birth revolved around my first son and new stepdaughter. How would this new baby change the dynamics of our family? Would my new daughter think I loved her less because of the connection I had with the babies grown in my belly? What about my first son? He had such a rough start with his biological father, how would it affect him when he no longer had me to himself? Would I treat my three children equally or scar them for life with my mistakes?

My husband was the available one for the first three months with my second baby, and I was the Mother to the oldest two. When he came home and went directly to the baby, my heart felt sad. What about me? I often felt frustrated with the baby's need for constant feeding, and I would cringe at his incessant cries. But, still, the feelings were different this time. My postpartum depression became softer, if you will. I was still a bit sad and worried, but I also felt true, all-encompassing love. Our family found our rhythm and the rest just sorted itself out.

I have never talked of those days to anyone.

RAGE SHOWS UP SOMETIMES

When we were already late, but I squeezed in forty-five seconds to run the vacuum, which coincidentally is enough time for both children (under 5 years old) to empty a bottle of baby shampoo onto the carpet in my bedroom. Rage showed up then.

She also showed up that time my youngest hurled her dinner plate to the floor — with a dead-panned look on her face. This was after I excused the cluttered surfaces in the kitchen so I could execute dinner, which was already twenty minutes late due to a tantrum by the oldest — and subsequent wetting accident. **Cleaning up piss and hot supper all at the same time.**

And she showed up when I tried to make my bed that day — you know how they love when you throw the sheet out, and it floats down to the bed in the bright sunshine? Rage was with me again.

Every day rage accumulates like little drops into a bucket that eventually spills over and floods us all. **I keep forgetting to try screaming into a pillow.**

The feeling is beginning to circle back once every few weeks. I'm afraid to admit it because I'm not sure how normal it is, but when she's with me, I'm paralyzed. I'm stiff. My throat closes. I can't blink. I see white. But there's no pause button with two small children in a flood. If I separate myself and shut the door, I can still hear them and, in fact, they only get worse when I walk away. For me, the idea of my children internalizing MOM WALKING AWAY feels worse. So I force it directly.

I restrain my daughter's little, but strong flailing body, in my arms which are flooded with rage. I hold her tight. Swaddled, like she wants to be. My body becomes a rigid container, with her as my tender center until she at least stops the screaming. Sometimes I scream too. I know I'm using my physical strength to dominate her, to assert my control over her, because isn't that what she wants in that moment? Isn't it what she needs? It seems to be the only thing I can do to bring her back. It's the only thing that seems to work.

What's worse are the things I've imagined during my "mom rage." What are these thoughts? Where do they come from? Am I a monster? I don't know what's safe. I don't know who I can talk to about this.

We both end in tears, first her, then me. We talk about it. We hold each other. We are sorry.

WHO WILL HOLD ME?

In my last month of pregnancy, I wondered where my friends were. Busy with their business and not inviting me to their fun. I guess due to my "circumstance."

Nobody asked how I was doing.

Nobody knew how I cried, how scared I was, or about the nightmares of my baby dying inside me. I guess, everyone just assumed I was happily waddling through life.

Until my due date, then the texts came. "Are you having contractions?"

Some days, the answer was **"No."** In which case, they responded. "What's up? Are they going to induce you?"

Sometimes the answer was **"Yes."** In which case, they celebrated my pain.

Confused, the days went on. I waited, wondering in my own anxiety and anticipation if anyone would ask, **"How are you??"**

Then one fateful day, it started. It was agony. Like a train wreck inside my body. It brought up repressed labor memories from my first son — even as different as it was.

I pushed so hard for two hours my nose bled, and I puked with every contraction; my body shook as my temperature dropped. My baby's heart began to race. But finally, with one final push, he was here!

And then people I hadn't heard from for months began to text: **"When can I hold your baby?"** and **"What day can I come?"**

"What day is it?" I thought, as I hobbled around, too sore and swollen to move or pee.

"Who will hold me?" I wondered, thinking of traditional times of families and villages that would care for the mother. A sisterhood of red tent understanding the six weeks of bleeding and crying postpartum.

My partner was wonderful in all the ways a man can be wonderful. Although he was there, he would never understand where I was, what had happened to me, what I had lost in those hours.

I so desperately wanted a friend to ask how I was, to acknowledge the trauma and not just the outcome.

I have come to realize many of my friends, these beautiful and strong women, never had a chance or allowance to process their births, other than reciting a story from the outside perspective.

And that I wasn't alone. There was a moment when puking, bleeding, grunting, and pushing, that I had felt my grandmothers there — where I was connected to every woman and mother that has ever been.

LEARNING AND UNLEARNING

"Mothers cannot help but be in touch with
the most difficult aspects of any fully lived life.
Along with the passion and pleasure, it is the
secret knowledge they share. Why on earth
should it fall to them to paint things
bright and innocent and safe?"

— JACQUELINE ROSE

——— • ———

DISCOVERING WHO I AM AGAIN

My nurse on the day we left the hospital: **"Isn't it amazing? It's like your heart left your body and is now in the world,"** she said.

This sentiment is so wildly beautiful, but triggered a vulnerability that I have never known. Being a mother has been the most terrifyingly amazing thing I have ever done. Being the mother of a 3-year-old makes motherhood feel brand new all over again, and I bet you can say that in every stage of parenting. Not only am I learning about this new life before my eyes, but I am discovering who I am again.

HEAR YOU, HEARING YOU

We have a funny saying in our home: "hear you, hearing you." It's the not-so-subtle reminder that your children will repeat everything they hear you say and do, including your mannerisms and responses. It's a reminder to model appropriately, especially when they are young.

Now, as a parent to a 14-year-old and 12-year-old, I have the fly-on-the-wall experience of listening to them. My son lowers his voice and squares his shoulders, cracks self-deprecating jokes. My daughter takes charge in small groups and asks who would like to speak next. She has analytical, one-on-one conversations with her teacher. Points her pencil at the screen. Thoughtful.

If it weren't for a pandemic, I wouldn't have the opportunity to "hear them, hearing them" like I did when they were little, and we were together like little mirrors all day. Now I see them reflecting me less, instead they reflect who they have become and who they are becoming, and they bounce their light off the rest of the world. They are a better me than I ever was.

CHI CHI

My daughter discovered a tampon in an old purse of mine and said, "I know what this is for. Girls put them up their butts to keep babies from falling out!" When I told her what they are really for, she replied, "Oh noooo I am NOT putting that up my chi chi."

DUMB VAGINAS

When my daughter was about 4, she finally noticed that her dad's parts were different than hers. We were taking a family sauna, and she pointed at him and said, "Papa's vagina is dumb."

THEY HAD TO SEDATE HER

I work in the deli at Hannaford. I am in the chicken room breading chicken tenders for the kitchen. **I hear the air pump continuously inhale and exhale.** I have tears running down my cheeks because not even a week ago, my daughter tried to take her own life by overdosing on her anti-depressants. They had to sedate her and put her to sleep to flush out her system. She was hooked to breathing tubes: the machine was helping her breathe, inhaling and exhaling. Watching her chest fall up and down as it was breathing for her. I wanted to crawl inside her mind and tell her that life is worth living and that she is so strong and can get through this hump in the road. But all I could do was hold her hand and physically be with her at the moment. I have never felt so helpless as a parent.

"The old definition of mother doesn't

ring true enough."

— GLENNON DOYLE

——— • ———

BUT FUCK THAT!! I'M LETTING THESE PANTIES SAG

Listen, I never liked kids before having my own. I never cared about childhood development. I never knew babies were whole humans that deserved respect. I thought kids were just side characters, you know? That's how they're always portrayed on television and in movies. And maybe that's how I was treated growing up — just an afterthought. A child to be seen and not heard. When I cried, I was told that I was wrong to be sad. I was distracted by my mom — "Don't feel that way — feel this way instead because it makes me more comfortable." I was made fun of for the reasons I was upset.

And you never fully get the true picture of your own childhood until you parent your own child (in whatever way that looks). I've learned Becky Bailey's conscious discipline. I'm an eager student of Janet Lansbury. And what it comes down to is that I want my children raised in a home that doesn't get scared of big feelings. A home where we learn how to express big feelings in a safe way. A home that has reasonable, consistent boundaries.

I've cried so many times because — what I'm saying to my child are things I never heard as little baby me: "I'm sorry", "I love all of you", "I'm here for you", "You spilled your drink, that's okay", "Yell it out baby, I've got your back." Never in my wildest dreams did I think that having children would open up my old childhood wounds. Wounds, I thought were badges. **Wounds I wore as armor.** Wounds that have been left unattended because I didn't even know I was cut to begin with! I was raised to pull my big girl panties up and fuckin' deal with it. But fuck that!! I'm letting these panties sag, y'all... I'm letting 'em slide all the way the fuck off. I'm going full-on commando. I'm letting the harshness I was raised in roll off of me as I hold an umbrella over my kids' heads.

You're safe with me, my babies. You're safe, you're safe, you're safe.

BEING A MOTHER
FILLS ME WITH FEAR

My childhood was filled with intense emotional and physical abuse.

My mother was a single mom in the 80s. My mother was mentally ill, undiagnosed, and unsupported, we lived welfare check to welfare check, in Section 8 housing. I wish I could tell her story with a happy ending; I wish it was a triumphant tale about overcoming adversity. It wasn't, she never received the help she deserved.

My brother and I lived in a war zone. Her instability, mania, and subsequent abuse changed us on a cellular level. She taught us the world was unsafe, which made it difficult to learn in school. We were her secret keepers, and we kept our own dark secrets. We loved her because that's what children do; we learned to hate ourselves because she told us we were the reason her life wasn't better.

I dreamt of adulthood. I daydreamed the way a prisoner is singularly focused on the day they are released. To feel the sun on my face. Break chains. Nobody would ever touch me in anger again, nobody could ever say cruel things to me again. One day I would be free.

I would be childless and free.

I decided I would never have children because the darkness of another can get planted inside you; it can grow and bear strange and bitter fruit.

I read studies, articles, and books on surviving child abuse.

I knew the odds were not in my favor. I was a victim poised to become a perpetrator.

I wanted desperately to break the silence; I began to tell war stories to anyone who would hear me. I wore my pain like a metal of honor. I made connections with those who had also suffered the pain of being a broken child. We were a tribe of lost children wearing grown-up clothes and moving through the adult world.

We soothed each other and congratulated each other's survival instinct. I thought that somehow these exchanges had healed me.

I fell in love; I became a mother twice, to two beautiful boys.

Being a mother fills me with fear, even now that my oldest is in his twenties. I am a fearful parent. I struggle with intimacy in my parent-child relationship. I can be a distant mother at times. I'm never violent, I'm careful never to be truly angry. But it's very hard to be a mom when your inner child needs a mother desperately. When you never learned to trust and therefore you can't trust yourself. It's hard to be a mom when the word MOTHER – somewhere in your psyche, terrifies you.

The wound that I thought I could self-heal in my twenties still bleeds daily. My sons teach me so much about love every day. I see my small self in them; it's through their innocence and purity that I finally can truly see myself, the little self. She is so sweet, I'm learning to love her.

MY PARTNER DESERVES IT.
I DO TOO.

I did the single parent deal, and the "force it to work because we have a kid" situation. I made multiple attempts over the first six years of my son's life to co-parent with his birth father, unsuccessfully. I was relieved when he decided to move to the states and lose contact.

When I met B, I was over the moon to share the journey of parenting with someone so deeply in touch with the complexity of relationships. He was kind and patient and emotional; receptive and open to trying new things. **The three of us melded together and became a family quickly and effortlessly.** So when we decided to expand our family to four, seeing eye-to-eye was the last thing I expected to be challenging.

All I ever wanted with my first child was to parent with someone equally passionate about raising him. I expected us to join forces and super-parent from the get-go. Yet suddenly, we were disagreeing on sleeping arrangements, how to parent our older child, nitpicking one another about small mistakes, and miscommunicating. Staying on the same page shifted from something we'd never had to work for, to something we had to work for — Every. Single. Day.

Our daughter is healthy and our family genuinely thriving. But communication takes work. Some days it's hard to not feel burnt out, exhausted from the effort it takes to see from his point of view. It's hard to stay compassionate and patient and fair. It's hard to not become resentful and stubborn I just want to scream sometimes, "MY WAY! This way works. I don't care what you think; I don't care that it makes you uncomfortable!" And I know that's not true... I do care. I care so much. I care more about his thoughts and feelings on the matter than anyone! **Between the hormones and having done it all alone the first time around, it's hard not to isolate myself and do it all alone again.** It's heartbreaking, really.

But I'll keep working on it. My partner deserves it. I do too. And especially our children. They deserve to experience both their parents' input. **I want them to witness two people leaning into the discomfort of relearning how to parent themselves and their children.** I want them to feel inspired to do the work too, to keep showing up even when it's not how you thought it would look.

CURING APPENDICITIS WITH A GARDEN HOSE

Two summers ago, my 11-year-old complained about a stomachache. We had been suffering a heat wave, multiple days of 95 degree or higher temperatures, so I thought he was just dehydrated from not eating and drinking enough. We were about to head to the lake to celebrate Fourth of July, but he insisted something wasn't right. Because it was hot, I took him to the backyard and soaked him with the garden hose. That's what you do in a heatwave, right?

It wasn't long after we arrived at the lake when he started vomiting. I was still convinced that this was a stomach bug that would pass, and our Fourth of July party would go on as planned. Finally, after thirteen hours of vomiting and doubled over in pain, he convinced me to take him to the emergency room. At 5:15 am on the Fourth of July, he was headed into surgery for appendicitis.

I will forever go down as the **mother who sprayed my child with the garden hose to cure appendicitis.**

DENYING MYSELF
AND EXCUSING OTHERS

During my pregnancy, my husband got to choose to sleep in or stay up late, but my exhausted body didn't have a choice. I would fall asleep when I didn't want to, and wake up way too many times throughout the night.

After the baby is born, women have more support, but it still feels like we don't get to choose many things, especially if we decide to breastfeed. Women often think, **"Either I suffer or my baby suffers."** So, of course, we choose to suffer for as long as we can handle it. I continue to say "Yes" to everyone and "No" to myself – regularly denying myself and excusing others.

I'm learning. Now when my kid comes up and asks for something I say, "I'm busy right now. Ask your dad." Even if I'm just reading a book! Sometimes I say it nicely and sometimes I say it differently, especially if I'm doing something for the benefit of the whole family. I'll say, "Do you see me making dinner/cutting the dog's nails/on the phone making a doctor appointment/bleeding on the side of the road? Do you see your father sitting on the couch? Now, go ask him for help!!" I have more of a choice than I think.

POOP SMEARED

When my son was about 8 months old, he needed a tub and I needed a shower. He enjoyed playing in the water, so I put him in his Bumbo seat, made for babies who can't yet sit up independently, and let him play while I took a shower. I grabbed some soap and started scrubbing baby from the bottom up, and quickly discovered not only had he pooped in his seat, but I had smeared poop all over his backside in the process of washing him. It was awful. Of course, I was the only one home, so no help from the husband!

I HAVE TWO BUTTS

Around age 3, my daughter asked me why girls have two butts.

"We don't have two butts, just one," I said.

"I have two. My little butt (her vulva) and my big butt back here," she explained.

That's when I realized she needed to know all the names of her anatomy....

"So what's this right here?" she asked.

"That's your clitoris."

"Oh! It's so cute!"

CAN I SEE YOUR VAGINA?

"Mom, can I see your vagina?!"

"No honey."

"Ok, Momma, it's beautiful."

THE DEATH OF A FUTURE I THOUGHT I WAS GOING TO HAVE

There is nothing like being a mother. Our stories are unique and should be honored as such. If we don't, many vulnerable women will feel alone and like they are not doing enough. Life is challenging for all women, and **there will always be a place where we can share our stories.**

There was a time before I had my son when I didn't know if my partner wanted a kid. There was a miscarriage. And, for a few months, there was the death of a future I thought I was going to have.

Later, after my son was born, even though I had been an early childhood educator, I truly had no idea what it meant to be a parent. The death of self happens as your child's life begins. **As your children get older, you slowly find your way back to a new you.** I would say that those who experience the death of a close one might experience a similar death of reality.

Being a mom is hard; it is a singular experience that is only understood if you've been a present mother. Know that YOU are enough.

LOST AND FOUND BODY PARTS

You would never think motherhood would involve so much losing and finding of my kids' body parts! Not to mention the body parts I've adamantly fought for them to retain, despite pressure otherwise: foreskin and adenoids, check!

The first body part went missing when my daughter was about a week old. It was her belly button. I'd been conscientiously trying not to pop it off. I respected its own timeline of shriveling up and doing whatever it needed to do next. But I'd also grown fond of it, and when it was suddenly gone during a diaper change, I became frantic. My husband, who also changed diapers, said he had no clue of its whereabouts, and didn't understand my concern. **"But, it was just there!!"** I cried, feeling like I'd lost of piece of my precious, new, daughter — albeit shriveled and strange. (The belly button, not my daughter — though she was kind of shriveled and strange at that point too.)

Imagine my surprise when pulling her cloth diapers out of the washing machine, I found her belly button, fully rehydrated like a gelatinous sea creature emerging from the depths! I ran to show my husband this discarded gummy worm of a body part. **"I found it, I found it! I found her belly button!"** I declared victoriously. "Gross, what are you going to do with it now?" he said. Well, I couldn't just throw away this lost and found treasure. I let it dehydrate in the fridge and then put it in a basket that would soon accompany hair clippings, lost teeth, and other artifacts of childhood.

A few years later, there was also a tooth that should have made it into that basket, but made it into my mouth instead. The first few teeth your children lose seem like a big event — to you and to them, (and to the tooth fairy, of course). But after a while, you literally can't keep track, teeth are falling out left and right. You are lucky if the tooth fairy can scrounge enough change (or God forbid, dollar bills) to keep the exchange of body parts for cash going.

Apparently, my daughter lost a tooth at school and brought it home in a ziplock bag in her lunch box. Somehow, she failed to mention that she'd lost that tooth (no big deal). So when I absentmindedly cleaned out her lunch box, I put the otherwise clean looking ziplock bag in the top drawer to be used again. At least that is what I figured I must have done a few weeks later, when I bit down into a cucumber and discovered a tooth in my mouth. I don't know if you have ever bitten down on a tooth that's not your own, but it's a very strange feeling. Your mind does a lot of things to figure out WHOSE TOOTH IT IS? Of course, you think it's your own, but when you are positively sure you STILL HAVE ALL OF YOUR OWN TEETH in your mouth, it's slightly disturbing to shout to your co-workers, "WHOSE TOOTH IS IN MY MOUTH?!" Needless to say, I finally figured it out.

Like I said, who knew so much of motherhood would involve lost and found body parts?!

"Our baby gives herself to me completely. There is no hesitation, no reservation, no holding back, no coldness, no craft, no tremor or fear in her love. Although our relationship may encompass tears, frustration, even fury, it is an utterly reliable bond."

— Louise Erdrich

——— • ———

ONE IS PERFECT, THE OTHER IS TWO

I thought mothers loved all their children the same?

Well, I'm just going to say it, but I think I have a favorite. All I know is one child is perfect, and the other child is two.

When I hold my second baby, 5 months old, I am in a blissful, dreamy world of only she and I. She looks at this version of my current self (tired, feeble, and visibly worn at the edges) with pure ecstasy. She lights up at even a side glance from me. She makes my insides swell and I pour myself even more into her. She brings me back to life. My 2-year-old, just isn't my favorite version of herself so far. Is that fair?

We run our days on my toddler's schedule. Because, honestly, there is no other way. Only after all of her doll babies have been perfectly wrapped in their respective blankies, only after I refill her milk, only after I soak up the pee from the carpet, only after I intercept the last toy she flung directly at the window — is when I get to escape to the baby bliss of my second daughter. **And if only for a few moments, she saves me from the other.**

Yes, I'm all read up on Janet Lansbury and Magda Gerber. I get it. But this is about me and the deep feelings of unconditional love for one child and the twelve hours of evasion, negotiations, and defensive tactics that are vital to keep myself semi-sane and the baby safe. This is beginning to feel like war, each and every day, and I'm in survival mode. Can I blame it on the pandemic?

RAZOR RASH IN
THE NETHER REGIONS

When my daughter was about 4, we took the kids camping. One morning, she and I headed to the community shower room to clean up.

Previously, I had found an old disposable razor stashed in our camper and (desperate times) earned myself a horrible razor rash in the nether regions.

As I opened the curtain to step out and grab my towel, my daughter yelled loudly, **"Oh my God, Mom!! YOU HAVE BUMPS ALL OVER YOUR PEE PEE!!"** I didn't know whether to die laughing, die of humiliation, or choke her out in the shower stall. She wasn't wrong, and I was mortified! Freaking kids.

HEY BABE

Chloe, age 3, after telling her she was going to be a big sister: "Would you like a little sister or a little brother?"

"Hmmmm, how about a cat?"

Also, my son called me **"Babe"** for a solid year 'cause that's what my husband calls me.

CONVERSATIONS WITH MY SEVEN-YEAR-OLD

"I need a bandaid."

"For what?"

"My knee."

"What's wrong with your knee?"

"I'm afraid it's going to faint."

:: After watching Bill & Ted's Excellent Adventure ::

"Were all those people from a long time ago real?"

"Well, the people in the movie were just actors, but yes, they were playing people who really lived a long time ago."

"What about the knight girl, was she real?"

"Yes, Joan of Arc led the French into battle when she was just a teenager."

".... that doesn't sound very safe."

"You are right. It was not."

:: Trying to wake them up this morning ::

"Just one more minute of sleep!"

"No, I already gave you one more minute, you need to get up."

"Fiiiive more minuuuuuuuutes!"

"You're negotiating in the wrong direction, kid."

"Can I have a free trial?"

"What?"

"Can I have a free trial?"

"Of what?"

"OF SLEEP!"

MY DAUGHTER LIED

My daughter lied. My sweet, quiet, honest (wasn't she?!) daughter lied. And not just a little lie, but a big one — the kind with real-world consequences.

Frustrated and confused, I wondered to myself, blood boiling: **"Is this what being the mother of a teenager feels like?!"** But, having been like her in my youth, compassion and empathy seeped in.

This is new territory for her as well as me as her mother. She is searching for who she is, navigating relationships, and finding her place. She's curious about sex. Thinking about the future, but very much in the here and now. She's becoming a woman and being a girl at the same time, wanting freedom from an adult but less chores than her younger siblings. Being a teenager can be lonely yet liberating. You feel wise but are confronted so often with shortcomings; I remember.

Because I remember, I try to pause, try to have difficult conversations, try to be transparent, and admit my shortcomings. I try to give her space to ask questions and let her know questions are safe to ask. I stumble through the conversations I longed for as a young girl, when my questions were answered with a curt "Because I said so." I wanted to be gently pulled in with an **"I'm here for you, you are loved, and you are forgiven."** This is also what I want for my daughter now. As a mother of a girl-becoming-a-woman, I must re-parent myself too; letting go of old patterns and embracing new challenges.

These years are good. Teenagers are not the awful, self-obsessed, lazy things to manage like the world may try to tell you. They are a gift. They will teach US if we make the time and effort to listen. They are fun. They are worthy of the same respect we, as adults, often demand. They are the future of our world. And WE get to be their mothers. What a responsibility and privilege it is.

"The sea, it is said, is like a mother. The salt water, the pulse and surges of the current, the magnified beat of your heart, and the muffled sounds reverberating through the water together recall the womb."

— LISA SEE

——— • ———

MY MOTHER IS
A GRANDMOTHER NOW

My mother is a grandmother now she says to me let's catch up so I put my book down take a deep breath say sure and she is already saying I've been thinking about you lately about how you are focused on the negative always you show your son anger and sadness you even (gasp) name it but where oh where is the joy and I try not to fly into space I say except in the 59 minutes each hour we experience it together and she is already saying well I suppose he is unusually happy but last week he had a nightmare and I say yes trying to will my feet onto the floor and she says and you let him watch television and I say yes and I am digging in my toes and she is saying so you agree you should stop what you're doing put him to sleep in my house in my bed every night because he's better off here and I give myself one last push down and I say well I wouldn't mind not being tired for a while and she says why don't you tell him how happy he is especially when he is unhappy it will make his anxiety better and I feel myself becoming a black hole I hear myself saying because that would be cruel and she says this is not an attack on you but literally all my thirty years of training and experience say you're doing it wrong and I say this is not an attack on you but I am a lifelong student of cruelty and she says you can't mean that and I say I do and I am gone.

TRUSTING A THREE-YEAR-OLD IS HARD.

I've got a kid that hangs back. She buys her time when it comes to new places and faces (or old ones, frankly). She watches. Assesses. She'll ease in with careful steps and hesitation. If something knocks her down early, it's going to be a while before she musters up the confidence to go again. Turns out, no amount of encouragement, discussion, bribery, or force will speed her process. Trusting a 3-year-old is hard. It doesn't suit my nature. I want to show her, teach her, let her know incessantly that she is capable, and make her try and try again. But I'm learning to swallow all of that. Watch. Support without telling. Trust. Her accomplishments are her own. Can a baby know what's right for her? She can.

I'M HELPING RAISE THIS WHOLE VILLAGE

"I want my mama," she wailed through her tears. But her mama wasn't nearby. I offered her a hug, and she melted into my arms. I carried her to a grassy spot in the sun and we sat down together and cuddled until she was ready to rejoin her friends. After a few minutes, she ran back to them, ready to play again. When I became a mama, I expected that I would have countless moments like these with my child. **But raising a child means also getting to know their friends and becoming a part of those children's lives as well.** And as the years pass, I've realized that I am not just raising one child, I'm helping raise this whole village. To all of you helping us to raise this next generation, whether you have your own kiddos or not, thank you, we love you, and we couldn't do this without you.

"Women without children are also the best of mothers, often, with the patience, interest, and saving grace that the constant relationship with children cannot always sustain."

— LOUISE ERDRICH

——— • ———

GRIEVING SOMETHING THAT I NEVER HAD

After touching base with my new neighbor, I realized I was grieving something that I never had.

She was mourning the news of the loss of her fertility.

She was kissing her chances of "natural" motherhood that her newly "mothered" friends had recently become exclusive about. **They made it clear the only motherhood they held true was one that included gestation.**

She was mourning the loss of her soon-to-be-gone uterus and her chances of bringing a human into the world whose genetic traits might remind her of the mother she lost last year.

At the moment, my instinct was to encourage her to focus on how much better she would feel sans the uterus that made her feel like a shell of herself. That's what I had done. Of course, I hugged her and said I could be her motherless friend. I shared that my fertility also had to be given up for my own life to continue. That night over dinner, it hit me. **I had never truly mourned my loss.**

Despite the fact that I had never had the desire to become pregnant, it was hard. Yet I found hope in the fact that I do love children, and motherhood isn't just about genes and gestation and pushing or going under the knife. I didn't have to mourn the loss of my own "potential" to become a mother at all. There were still plenty of chances at that.

It is heartbreaking when women promote the idea that motherhood is unattainable without growing your own baby. My friends who held those ideas are gone. Mourning those lost friendships is more like a celebration. I choose to birth supportiveness and inclusion. I am fertile and ripe with a love and strength that isn't dependent on DNA.

IT WAS A SHOCK TO ME

It was a cool November morning. I was cleaning up the kitchen after breakfast while my 2 ½ year-old and 16-month-old daughters played on the kitchen floor at my feet. With my hands in the hot, sudsy water, I leaned into the countertop and felt a familiar thump, thump in my belly. "Maybe just a spasm?" I thought to myself. I had just started introducing table food to my daughter while breastfeeding full-time, and still had a bit of my baby belly. I was in the throes of a difficult marriage; sex was far from my mind most of the time. I had not yet started menstruating since my daughter's birth and had faithfully used a diaphragm on the few occasions of intimacy. I couldn't possibly be pregnant. Right?

Later that week, I called to set up an appointment to see my doctor. During that visit, I discovered that I was 5 ½ months pregnant. It was a shock to me.

My beautiful baby boy was born on February 4, 1978. He was perfect in every way, long and lanky at 24" and 7 lbs, 8 oz. I signed us out of the hospital and took him home when he was 4 hours old, as I didn't have the luxury of health insurance. It was the third time I had decided to avoid a hospital stay. I knew what I was doing.

My son was an extremely bright baby but slept, on average, four hours in any 24-hour period. I was exhausted with no sleep and three babies, but so are many mothers. I breastfed him exclusively, but even at 3 and 4 months old, he was so distracted that I could only keep him at my breast for a few minutes. He would wrestle away from me to see everything around him. At 6 months old, he could barely reach the top crib rail with his little fingers, but he could still manage to lift himself out of the crib, drop to the floor with a thud, and make his get-a-way. He was walking confidently and beginning to run between 6 and 7 months. His athleticism was incredible. *It was a shock to me.*

Later, I watched him struggle in school, as the busy work bored him. He quickly became labeled, and then lived up to that "problem child" label. I used every resource I had, but I watched this handsome, athletic, gifted child failing to fit into society's required agenda. He was such a talented and perceptive boy. Surely he would find his way as brilliant and mechanically inclined as he was. (At age 5 he quickly mastered the Rubik's cube, pulled apart an electrical outlet — Argh! — and put together or took apart any other puzzle he could get his hands on.) Yet, every day felt like a struggle. I was desperate to help this boy I so deeply loved, but there was no help to be found. *It was a shock to me.*

In time, he developed into a kind and generous man, despite years of adversity and his inability to meet society's expectations in school, with relationships, and in his career. He passionately taught others about anything in which they showed interest. He had an insatiable appetite for learning, especially all things mechanical. He and I would spend hours discussing options for design and construction, remodeling and creating. His eyes would light up with brilliant ideas as we brainstormed. It gave us both such joy and connected our like minds.

As an adult, channeling his gift was difficult for him, but he most often used his ability to help anyone in need, even if it meant his own immediate obligations weren't met. He desperately sought reassurance that he was valued. Helping others who were grateful gave him momentary pride in himself. Daily he still struggled with insomnia and a brain that was so overactive that I could see the pain in his eyes. Alcohol became his answer to the pain and spinning, yet he continued on despite that destructive choice. He fathered two beautiful children. Relationships fell apart, but he built new ones. Jobs fell apart, but he would find another that excited him with the hope of a new opportunity. But things never lasted with this wonderful man. *It was a shock to me.*

February 1, 2017, the sheriff's car pulled up in our yard. The sheriff slowly walked to the front door and knocked. As he sat down in my living room, he told me he had to share some bad news for me. My son was found that evening. He had died of suicide by hanging. It was three days before he turned 39. *It was a shock to me.*

We held a gathering of family and friends on his birthday, February 4, 2017. Hundreds of people gathered to honor him. Everyone talked about how much they loved and respected him. Multitudes told of their gratitude for the endless kind and generous things he had done over the years. Those stories filled my heart with pride. My son chose to leave us and his pain behind, never having felt that love, value, and gratitude of and for him that was so apparent that day.

Our society needs to value all people even if we have to search hard to find their gifts. We need to be flexible in our expectations. We need to love people for who they are, just the way they are. We need to honor, respect, and care profoundly for all people. We have a very long way to go as a society. *It's all still a shock to me.*

THE GIFT

"And be REALLY CAREFUL, Mommie, it's REALLY BREAKABLE!" Alden handed me the little package as if it contained a bubble still swirling and pulsing with its break from the wand.

He'd saved it till last — till the cacophony of Christmas discovery was spent and had quieted into this moment — time to bring out — "The Gift."

"I picked it out ALL BY MYSELF," he beamed, climbing up on my lap to help me open it. **"It's REALLY FRAGILE, so be careful!"**

I quickly swung it out of the path of his flying foot.

He had just turned 5. He might as well have been my soul.

A few months before, I had made him a little green tadpole costume for Halloween, and we went trick-or-treating as a toad and tadpole. Soon after, he became my storytelling partner, performing Arnold Lobel and other classics for schools around the district.

As he settled onto my lap that Christmas, he looked up at me with a vibrant, bursting excitement — relishing my coming pleasure.

I savored the impetuous abandon of his joy, anticipation, and love for me.

The really fragile gift? That moment was for me. I remember and relive it, every time I use the little figurines that sit on my kitchen counter: pepper in the happy green sitting toad, and salt in the silly frog lying on its side with its foot in the air.

LOOK MUMMA, A JELLYFISH!

Our toddler was potty training. Like most kids her age, her interests in the sights and sounds from the wondrous world of the toilet bowl were piqued. Now everyone's toilet time was full of questions, comments, and friendly farewells down with a flush.

Since having children my flow has become much heavier. On day two of my period, I had to pee and right on cue, my bathroom broadcaster arrived at my knees.

The bright red gelatinous clots danced down the toilet bowl making the water look like a lively aquarium. I tried to be quick but she was quicker. She peered into the bowl and her face lit up like on Christmas, "Look Mumma! A jellyfish! It's a big momma jellyfish! She's so pretty!"

I couldn't argue with her, and for a moment I was totally charmed to stare in awe of my glorious menses with my daughter. It was pretty. I figured it's never too soon to smash stigmas, especially while building a more witchy matriarchy among ourselves.

MOMMA HELD IT DOWN

Grief is an old friend. Since I was a young girl, I've lost many friends and family members to an array of death's dealings: cancer, car accidents, overdose, and suicide. I know love and loss intimately, and until I became a parent, did not understand why I was chosen to experience so much grief. Grief visited me again as a new mother, and this is a glimpse of my story.

It was October 11, 2017. Twelve days before our child's first birthday. I had just started school and was taking my first big exam, when I got a call from my brother's lover. "I can't find Darren," she said on the other end of the line.

Darren had died; by his own hand and was found by my partner. Our child's first birthday was shrouded in sorrow. We were lucky to have so many loved ones surrounding us. Darren's death was a great community loss, but for us, it was the death of a chosen family member, a brother, an uncle, and a kindred spirit. **The heaviness of his death overshadowed my child's first birthday,** but we chose joy and celebrated, anyway. The intimate way that I know grief allows me to cherish the small moments of joy that surround us. In retrospect, I wanted more than anything to have only joy on my son's first birthday. But we only move forward.

As time went on, my partner held it together, for the most part. He would share with me glimpses of his pain, but the sorrow was looming. He would share with me that he was having flashbacks. These began to happen more frequently, and my partner took to alcohol to soothe his pain. That worked until he got into an accident at work at the beginning of the Covid pandemic. There was an explosion in a small space, and he burned his hands and face. After that, my partner's downward spiral became unbearable and unsafe for our family. I gave him an ultimatum, **"Get help... quit drinking... or we are moving out."** My partner chose life. He shared with me dark secrets, quit drinking, and we've been going to therapy. He took the reins and here we are.

I know grief now more intimately than many, and as I share this experience I wonder, was the cumulative grief meant to serve as a buffer to hold this pain for myself, my partner, and my child? Was I meant to grieve many losses so that I could bear witness to my partner's pain without judgment? So that my son could see that Momma HELD IT DOWN? So that he could see what love looks like in all its rawness? So he could understand that when you love someone you stand by them, steadfast in your self-respect and boundaries, while guiding the person you love through the dark? I don't know. Maybe.

Grief and parenting simultaneously challenged me to the core. From both parenting and grief, I learned that it's not one day at a time, but minute-by-minute and play-by-play. I learned that I am really good at being comfortable with discomfort. I have a well that runs deep with patience, but that well has its limits. Forgiveness is a priority, and it might be the hardest thing I've ever done when head-to-head with running away.

Self-care sometimes means just washing your face. Gratitude, oh sweet gratitude. You are the soul that soothes the savagest of beasts. Nature has real magic. **When loneliness sets in, reach the fuck out.** True friends just listen. Parenting means sitting down and crying with your child when they are throwing it down. Holding the line is really, really hard, and flexibility is everything.

OUR MOTHERLOAD

"Young women today will come of age

with fewer rights than their mothers and

grandmothers."

— Justice Stephen Breyer,

Sonia Sotomayor, And Elena Kagan,

Dissenting Opinion, Roe V. Wade Overturn

June 25th, 2022

——— • ———

HE WANTED TO GET ME PREGNANT WITHOUT MY CONSENT

My first abortion was at 24, when I was living in Oregon. I found out at about 8 weeks. I had no money, a gig job, and lived across the country from everyone I knew. It took me one day to file for help from the state and receive it. **From finding out I was pregnant, to going in for the abortion pills, took three days. I have never felt any regret.**

Let's skip ahead some years. When I was 31, I entered an abusive relationship that had a hold on my life for two years. At the end of the relationship, when all was going to hell, my abuser told me he wanted to get me pregnant and had been trying without my consent. We broke up, and I found out I was pregnant seven weeks later.

At this time, Kansas had only two abortion clinics in the whole state, and no funding.

Luckily, I had the support of friends that got me through the second abortion. I went in for the in-clinic operation, which took about ten minutes. I felt relief after it honestly, knowing that bringing a child into the world when I was again, not financially able and in a toxic relationship, would only create harm.

I want women to know there is solidarity out there.

MY BODY FELT DIFFERENT IMMEDIATELY

Storytelling is my love language, and you'd think that I'd be able to be loud and proud over this, but as you know or can imagine, it's all very complicated. I've never shared this publicly; I probably should, but for now, I'll share it with you.

I had an abortion when I was 22, living in Portland, OR in the early '00s. It was after a big fight with a girl I thought I was in love with, and I got too drunk, partied with the wrong folks, and had an encounter that I barely remember, definitely did not consent to, with a dude whose name I doubt I even knew. My body felt different immediately, and although I didn't take a test for a couple more weeks, I knew it would be positive.

My life was in a downward spiral. My mom had died about a year prior to this; I was abusing drugs and alcohol, was barely employable, and had lost my car because I couldn't pay to get it out of tow. I made an appointment with Planned Parenthood, having no idea how I would come up with the money for the procedure.

I was scared and alone.

I borrowed money from my dad, told him it was for my car, and took the bus to PP on the day of my appointment. I had a friend pick me up, and we didn't talk about anything on the way home.

I wanted kids but couldn't imagine doing it without my mom. I've never had kids or any more pregnancies. I sometimes wonder if that was my only chance, and I wasted it because I was a mess of a person. I have never regretted it; just curious and maybe sad sometimes.

Thank you for giving me the space to put this out into the universe and **maybe give a little love to my younger self.** And a lot of gratitude for the fact I had a choice.

ABORTION WAS ILLEGAL
IN MY STATE

I was 15 years old, "in love," and thought it was a long term relationship as many young girls feel. I grew up in a household of gentle, kind and honorable men and had not experienced distrustful people in my life. I trusted, just as I had been taught by family. I believed what I was told and took things at face value.

I skipped a couple of periods and knew I was probably pregnant. I went to have the big conversation with him. During that conversation, he shared that he was also dating another girl who was also pregnant (she was younger than me). I was absolutely distraught and in shock. What about trust? Where was the honor?

With great trepidation, I finally found the courage to confide in my parents, which broke their hearts. Despite their emotional shock and pain, they immediately made an appointment with the OBGYN who had delivered me. They also consulted with our minister, who was a kind and progressive man and a great supporter of our family.

In 1970, abortion was illegal in our state, but the doctor made connections for us to travel to New York to have the procedure done. The boy's parents opposed the decision my parents, minister, and the doctor had made for me. Yes, that decision was made for me. I was a child.

I remember feeling as if I was in an emotional fog. I was mortified as I attended classes at my small high school as the gossip spread quickly. It appeared that everyone knew and was staring at me, and talking about me. When the appointed date came, my parents drove me to Utica, New York. I remember very little of the trip as I sat in the back seat and watched the landscape go by. Upon arriving at the clinic, I was taken into a procedure room alone. I remember separating myself from everything that was happening. To this day all that I remember is lying on the examination table, the paper underneath me, the paper gown I was wearing, and the cold stirrups. I was 14 weeks pregnant and weighed 95 lbs. I was a child, a very naïve child. I know the decision that was made was the best for me, but I still feel guilt and shame about it. Would I, could I ever trust again?

I have placed a small pink quartz stone on the grave of my son, who died by suicide at 39. It helps me grieve and remember. Two lives never, never to be forgotten.

NO WOMAN MAKES THIS DECISION LIGHTLY

Those who are "pro-life" should put their money where their mouth is, and adopt a baby of rape, incest, or drugs.

I am the first generation of women who could get contraception, without parental consent. This was in Baltimore, many years ago.

I am thankful that I never needed an abortion, which is thanks to Planned Parenthood.

I WAS DRUGGED

I was drugged and raped in college. If I hadn't miscarried I would have aborted. To this day I don't even talk about it with my husband because the experience was so horrifying that I just need to forget it all. I can't imagine raising the child of the person who did that to me, alone, and not being able to finish college or have all the experiences I had in my twenties. Now I'm a mother of two, the most wonderful experience of my life, but it's fucking hard. I have a solid marriage. We have good jobs. I have the support (physical, financial and emotional) from both sides of family. I really don't think I could have provided a healthy life for that child if I had been forced to.

"...from the very moment of fertilization, a woman has no rights to speak of. A state can force her to bring a pregnancy to term even at the steepest personal and familial costs."

"With sorrow — for this Court, but more, for the many millions of American women who have today lost a fundamental constitutional protection — we dissent."

— JUSTICE STEPHEN BREYER,

SONIA SOTOMAYOR, AND ELENA KAGAN,

DISSENTING OPINION, OVERTURN OF ROE V. WADE

— • —

I HAVE NEVER TOLD ANYONE ABOUT THIS

I had an abortion after my divorce. I slept with just about anyone I could because I felt empty. My daughter went to her dad's most weekends, **and I was a "free spirit."** I was on the pill. No idea who the dad was. When I didn't get my period, I freaked the fuck out and took a test. I stared at that test for 24 hours as I lay in bed puking and crying. I called a friend who immediately took action. She knew I barely wanted one child and that I definitely didn't want to raise another alone, not to mention what it would do to my parents. I went to an abortion clinic in Portland. I had to go in alone because they didn't allow anyone else. This was before cell phones were used widely, so my poor friend had to wait for me. I hated the procedure — not because of guilt about aborting cells from my body, but because I felt violated. They were kind and soft-spoken, but the procedure itself just felt yucky. **I never cried over that "baby" because it would have ruined my chances of giving the child I wanted, my daughter today, a life she deserved.** I was a poor teacher who couldn't get her own shit together. I have never told ANYONE about this. I know I should speak out, but my daughter is older now, and I don't want to open up old wounds that may change her opinion of me — not the abortion, but the fact I slept around.

NEITHER OF US FELT READY

We accidentally got pregnant right after getting engaged. Neither of us felt mentally, emotionally, or financially ready to have a baby. We weighed all of our options and abortion was the only one that made sense. If we had kept that child, we wouldn't be able to provide the life we're providing for our toddler now. It was a gut wrenching choice to make, but it was the only choice to make.

I can't imagine being in that situation and having no other option but to bring another life into the world. I loathe that my daughter will grow up with fewer rights and freedoms than I have experienced and benefited from. I'll also add that we got pregnant while I was on birth control. Lucky .1% in that one circumstance, I suppose.

I SQUATTED, REACHED INSIDE, AND...

We were interrupted unexpectedly, and he bolted out the back door so no one would know. The phone rings. On the other end was him. He said he couldn't find the condom. Um... What??? What do you mean you couldn't find it?? I rip apart the bed, throwing the sheets and blankets across the room. It was nowhere to be found.

Horrified at the only option left of where it could be, I headed to the shower. My inner self yelling at me, "No... surely it can't be lost in there. IS it?" The water ran over my shoulders as I felt to see if it was just kind of in there. Still nothing. I squatted, reached inside, and slowly pulled it out of my vagina with a long snap. I stared at it. The feeling of being sick to my stomach hit hard, and that odd sort of panic/relief laugh came over me... **Holy Shit... What the actual fuck? How did this happen??** So many questions ran through my mind; I was mortified and in shock... wrong size condom? Do I have a powerful pelvic floor? Did I suck the thing right off??? Am I going to get pregnant???

I pulled myself together and drove the store for Plan B. Who knows if that mishap would have turned into something more. Thank Science for modern medicine and the ability to get resources so easily. It did not drastically change my life because I was enjoying being sexual. I am sexual.

Each one of us has had our own nightmare, let's not take steps backward and accidents become what **we** have to live with.

My heart hurts for women who have to carry the burden of potential resources not being available.

SEXUALITY WAS SHAMEFUL

Growing up in a **southern baptist household,** sexuality was shameful — the only option was abstinence until marriage. Even though my family has significantly relaxed their beliefs over time, I don't think I will ever feel comfortable discussing the subject with them. I still struggle sometimes with the deeply entrenched shame related to body and sexuality.

When my little sister announced she was pregnant, I felt immense sadness along with my joy. The sorrow wasn't for her; she has a healthy and happy marriage, is financially secure, and lives close to family. No, I grieved because I would experience my dear sister's pregnancy only virtually from a great distance. I wished I could be the wise older sister who had been there before and could guide her along the way. I wanted to share stories and commiserate when she talked about her morning sickness.

I, too, had constantly felt nauseous when I was pregnant, and I understood what she was going through. **Only she didn't know I had been pregnant** — because I never told her and because I had an abortion. I was very fortunate to have easy legal access in a state where the right to choose is now more restricted. I don't regret the decision I made. I adore my little nephew, and my sister is now pregnant with a second child. While I don't think she would judge me for my choice, I'm not willing to risk other family members finding out. So again, I commiserate in silence, holding my secret close.

PREGNANCY OF AN UNKNOWN LOCATION

I was trying to get pregnant. I'm a planner and was thrilled to finally get a positive pregnancy test. Then there was bleeding — I had lost it. My good friend brought chocolate, wine and a whole lot of love when I told her. My husband was so thankful for her because there was no comfort in our loss. When my ovulation tests became whacky, **I took another pregnancy test which indicated I was still pregnant.** I came to learn it was a **"pregnancy of an unknown location."** Did you know your ovary doesn't connect to your fallopian tube? Did you know an embryo can attach to another organ in your abdomen? Neither did I.

As my non-viable pregnancy continued, I opted to have a chemo shot to stop the growth of cells (an abortion). My pregnancy hormones were dropping, so it seemed the chemo shot had worked — until it didn't. I woke up and collapsed, vomiting in pain. I was bleeding out. It was an ectopic pregnancy that ruptured my fallopian tube. I was rushed to the hospital and had emergency surgery to remove my fallopian tube which saved my life.

The emotional recovery was tougher than the physical recovery. I still hope to get the pregnancy I so dearly want. **Without abortion as healthcare, women with ectopic pregnancies and pregnancies of unknown locations will die.**

I MARRIED YOUNG AND BRIEFLY

As a college student in the early 1980s, I married young and briefly, and had two abortions. I trusted a man who turned out not to be trustworthy. I believed myself enough to know I did not want children with him, and that **I was not at all ready to have a family.** It was a time when abortion was legal and accessible, which now seems fortunate and precious, though I didn't realize it then.

TOO POOR

I had been engaged for about six months. I had been feeling ill for several weeks, when I missed a second period and became worried. (Because who on contraception worries about just one missed?) Despite having an IUD, I took a home pregnancy test. **When he came home from work that night, I had a surprise waiting for him.** Our immediate response was, "How soon can we get an appointment?" because there was no way we could afford to have a child on our meager combined income.

I got in at Planned Parenthood within a week, where I found out I was 13 weeks along. They removed my IUD and the embryo and inserted an arm implant with no fuss. I thought I was going to barf at the end of the procedure, but the assistant stuck a cup of peppermint extract under my nose, and I immediately felt fine.

I'm glad I was able to have such a quick, easy, and safe procedure done on short notice. I'm still hoping to be a mother sometime in the future when we're ready.

I WAS DEPENDING ON MY IUD TO WORK

I had just graduated college. I was 22 years old. Left my boyfriend. Had a fling. Learned I was pregnant. Not sure which guy. Fresh out of school, blasting into the the big world with big hopes and big dreams, it was TOTALLY NOT in my plan to settle down with a baby. I was depending on my IUD to work. But it failed. I felt like my body had an unwanted growth that needed to be removed. Luckily, my abortion was safe, quick, compassionate, supportive and trouble-free. What a relief! I never did have human children. I have no regrets.

I WAS TERRIFIED, ALONE, AND ASHAMED

It was 1969. A few months earlier, a man I was on a date with had forcibly raped me.

Now, I was in Australia at a college friend's sheep ranch living for six months when I needed emergency wisdom teeth extraction due to impaction and abscess. After the surgery, I woke up feeling wet in my genital area. **Three months later, I was visibly pregnant, despite not being sexually active.** Fortunately, my college friend's mother noticed and knew a lady in town, and she performed an abortion on me at her house. I was terrified, alone, and ashamed. I will never forget it to this day.

Thirteen years after that, I was happily married. We had two children.

"Let's stop telling moms to do better self-care.

Care is legalized abortion and paid family leave,

not a fucking bubble bath."

— MINNA DUBIN

——— • ———

I WANTED THAT BABY SO MUCH

I had a complete hysterectomy that removed my uterus and a baby with a healthy beating heart the night before Roe v. Wade was overturned.

My partner and I had been trying to get pregnant for two years, and when we gave up, it finally happened. We were excited but nervous. I started bleeding three different times and thought I was miscarrying each time. But every time they checked, it was still there, heart rate increasing. With all the early ultrasounds, they noticed it was implanted close to my C-section scar. Things started happening very fast, and suddenly I was sent to a specialist in Anchorage who confirmed my doctor's suspicions — **it was a rare ectopic pregnancy called a C-section scar ectopic.** The placenta grows into the scar tissue and ruptures the uterine wall, often in the first trimester.

My HcG levels were too high to end the pregnancy with a drug called Methotrexate, and a D&C (dilation and curettage) would have likely punctured my bladder. So on Friday morning, my pregnant body woke up without anything in it —

a sudden evacuation of a pregnancy

and everything that would let me try to have a baby again.

In the midst of all the ensuing sadness, I find myself incredibly thankful to live in a time and place when this condition can not only be detected, but also that I was able to have a procedure that would save my life. Providence Hospital had to approve this through their ethics board because they are a Catholic institution, and I am thankful that they respected the urgency of the situation.

I wanted that baby so much, but I was so thankful for the abortion. Waking up the morning after surgery in a hospital and watching the fall of Roe v. Wade as I cried in pain and loss. I also felt relief that my childbearing years were over as the laws changed and I would never be forced into a situation I didn't want or that could injure me. I felt a great awareness of how lucky I was to have had my childbearing years fall in a period when women could make their own decisions regarding pregnancy. This week I spent a lot of time crying for myself, for my partner, and for all the women who now have to make scared and furtive decisions when they are at their most vulnerable. Thanks for giving me a space to share.

My mind screams: "How is this possible??"

I can not imagine the possibility of not being able to have the extraction with ~*Aaron's* pregnancy. The two-day wait was so unsettling. I just cannot.

This is why I wanted to share my story.

There is a need for abortions.

A need for safe healthcare for all who can conceive.

I OWNED THAT CHOICE

I was 23 when I had an abortion. I was a senior in college and getting ready to study and travel abroad for my final semester. I was planning to drive the Alcan Highway with my best girlfriend after graduation and felt my bright future and all the possibilities of life stretch before me.

My boyfriend of five years and I had been ignoring the sounding alarm of our ending relationship, hitting the snooze button for the better part of my last year in college. After another night pretending we could continue having sex without complicated emotions, I traveled to my childhood home for a weekend.

Arriving home with sore breasts and a gag reflex — I knew. **Before a drugstore test confirmed it, I knew I was pregnant, and my heart sank.** Telling my Catholic parents wasn't an option. I didn't want the lecture on adoption that was sure to come. We had never even talked about sex growing up, and I had sat through enough Sunday masses to understand what religion thought of women and motherhood.

When I called Planned Parenthood between my college courses that next week, I remember the kindness and calm of the woman on the other end of the line. Struggling with the crossroads I found myself at — the snatch of my future teetering in those hard moments — I remember her asking me if I wanted to have this baby. "No," I said in a whisper, "I can't give up the life I just started living, and I am afraid I would resent having to." **She told me I had a choice.** That it was my body and my life, and resenting a baby wasn't fair to myself nor the baby. I remain grateful to her and the moment I owned that choice.

Decades later, I am married with two incredibly, deeply cherished children. Children I planned for and felt ready for — mentally, emotionally, physically, and financially.

And even though I wanted these babies more than anything,

I sometimes feel pangs of resentment

at all that I have given up to be a mother.

MY JOY QUICKLY TURNED TO PARANOIA

I found out I was pregnant unexpectedly at 42! We were so excited; it was everything that I wanted. We have a 3-year-old, but I didn't feel complete.

When I told anyone we were pregnant, they would instantly talk about miscarriage, and **my joy quickly turned to paranoia.** Am I going to lose this baby? My doctor wouldn't see me till I was 10 weeks; it was the policy of the office. I was growing increasingly paranoid with all the miscarriage talk and lack of medical care. My husband called the office and asked them to see us sooner, but they refused and said if we wanted to be seen sooner, we could go somewhere else… so we did.

We saw the heartbeat at the first appointment. I felt much better. Two weeks later, I went to use the bathroom. When I wiped, there was blood, and my heart sank. I was losing the baby like everyone had said I would. The doctor said I could come for a heartbeat check two days from then. I knew it wasn't good. The next day we went to the hospital, and with my legs spread and a wand in my vagina, surrounded by four strangers, I was told, "Sorry, hun, there's no heartbeat." I never cried so much in my life.

I decided to miscarry naturally because I didn't know any better. I thought I had passed the baby, but the next day I took my daughter to soccer, and on the way home, I started having contractions and gushing blood. I got out of the car in my driveway, and blood poured down my legs. **I got myself and my 3-year-old in the house and went to the bathroom.** I had bled through my clothes. There was blood everywhere. I got in the tub; I was having contractions and bleeding heavily. I called the on-call doctor to ask for pain medicine, and he told me it would be over in a couple of hours. No meds needed. I guess he never miscarried naturally or felt the physical pain.

I laid in a tub filled with blood while my dog kept coming in and out. My daughter was asking why I pooped in the tub because she didn't know what blood was. I had contractions and clot passing for the next three days.

One week later, we took my daughter to Monster Jam at Gillette stadium. I started hemorrhaging when we got there, but out of mom guilt tried to stay awhile for my kid. My husband finally said we had to go and when I stood up blood poured out of me. I had to be rushed to the hospital by my husband and daughter. Evidently, when I had a sonogram the day before, there was still quite a bit of pregnancy in me — only that wasn't shared with me. At the ER, the rest of the pregnancy was pulled out of me with forceps and no pain medication, until I made them stop to give me some.

I have never heard anyone say, "We lost the fetus after a miscarriage." I saw a TikTok recently with a girl repeatedly saying *if the fetus is a baby how come a woman doesn't get food stamps while pregnant, if the fetus is a baby how come you don't get* blah blah blah.

My OBGYN office called me three weeks ago to schedule my c-section and I thought, "Wow, thanks for reminding me that we lost our baby." I burst into tears. There is no excuse. People thought I was crazy for suggesting that the doctor's office should take the time to cancel all future appointments after miscarriage, like "Oh, that's just how it is." If miscarriages are so common, why is this not a thing? We need to do better. Maybe one day women's voices will be important enough and it will be different.

THE ONLY THING TRAUMATIC WAS KEEPING IT A SECRET

My pregnancy test came back positive on my oldest child's birthday. I was stunned. I had been successfully using an IUD for many years. After watching me labor for days through my first childbirth, my husband promised he would get a vasectomy when we were done having kids. "It's the least I can do," he said. Then, when it was time, he chickened out. I have discovered that people will promise a lot when a child is born, but mostly it is the mothers who pick up the pieces. Anyway, I kept using my IUD. I probably should have harassed him more to have a vasectomy, but what can I say? **I believe in bodily autonomy.**

When we found out I was pregnant several years later, there were lots of feelings. We didn't want another baby, but we didn't know we'd be in this situation. We were also worried. Where was that IUD? Had it fallen out, or was it still in there? What sort of problem could that be for me or the fetus? An X-ray was not permitted because the affect on the fetus is unknown. We decided I would get an abortion. Because I'm older, I'm fairly in tune with my body and caught it quickly. I took the abortion pill around six-weeks. If I lived somewhere with a six-week ban, they could have disallowed it because it was close. I couldn't imagine mobilizing any quicker than I did. Anyway, I took the pills, and it was not traumatic or even painful. I was told not to look for the fetus because I wouldn't be able to see it with my naked eye. Of course, I looked but saw nothing but blood. I was a little sad thinking about what might have been, but mostly I was relieved and thankful.

The only thing traumatic about the experience was keeping it secret from so many who would have been angry and called me a murderer. I'm telling this story anonymously for that reason, but I want other women to know that they are not alone and that I will fight like hell for their reproductive freedom.

I'M SO SAD I WASN'T IN THE POSITION TO HAVE ANOTHER KID

I spent the first night of my son's life with only him in the hospital, as my husband was tired and needed to go home to sleep. I didn't have a lot of help or support from him.

My beautiful son was around 18 months old when I knew we hadn't been safe. I immediately went to the store and got the Plan B pill, but was still pregnant. **Then I knew I needed Plan C.** I went to Anchorage, and while my aunt helped watch my son, I tried to get an abortion. I couldn't. There were no options that didn't require some pre-planning.

I finally found a place in Kenai. I cried in the car because I had to stop breastfeeding my son and I didn't want this to affect his life. I knew my husband wasn't a helpful partner with one kid, I couldn't imagine two. I'm so sad I wasn't in the position to have another kid. I can't believe this choice is being taken away from us.

I FELT SAFE AND CARED FOR BY MY KIND-HEARTED DOCTOR

My partner and his first wife had a baby born with anencephaly (underdeveloped brain and incomplete skull). He held the baby, before she died thirty minutes later. The baby's death ended their marriage.

We wanted to have a baby together and worked with a fertility doctor for a year. The pregnancy was considered high-risk, although I had a natural birth at age 37. The doctor nor hubby made it in time, but that's another story.

Our second pregnancy resulted in omphalocele (baby's insides were on the outside, including liver). The doctor arranged for me to meet and talk to other parents whose baby had the same condition. He even arranged a no-cost flight to Seattle if I wanted another consult – I'm grateful for him.

My baby's omphalocele was substantial. I had my toddler.
His/our 9 yr old son had a brain injury a few years earlier and was involved in therapies. My hubby lost his fiancée in a car accident, lost a baby, and that marriage. How much grief and financial responsibilities could he withstand? I decided to abort.

It was thirty years ago when I went to that Anchorage clinic. There was a group of protestors outside... I remember a fat, white guy in front. The wait before the D&C was hard but inside, I felt safe and cared for by my kind-hearted doctor.

It was my choice. I protected my family.

TWO DIFFERENT CHOICES CAN EVOKE THE SAME EMOTIONS

When I found myself pregnant in a toxic relationship, I chose the "good girl" route, married him, and had the baby. What followed were years of heartbreak and abuse until I found my way out. Having my baby at that time was hard, but it was MY choice.

My friend's choice was different. She was single with three children, living on child support and a low-paying job. She was a true momma who loved her children ferociously and worked hard both physically and emotionally to build them a safe family. Unlike me, she did not have the support of parents who helped monetarily and with time who kept my baby often, making my adjustment easier. .

After a night of yearning for a little bit of freedom, my friend found herself pregnant. And, she made HER choice, to save her family and herself. I was there for the actual procedure, (waiting in the car because it was a hot topic at the time, and clinics were full of protests and unstable protesters), and I was there through the stages that followed.

Trust me when I tell you, an abortion is not casual, and the laws do not reflect what a woman goes through when choosing the option that would let her keep fighting for herself and her children.

It was hard to watch. I held her close for days as she worked through the **grief, anger, and acceptance.** It was far from a casual decision that some think overturning Roe v. Wade will change. Sometimes the decision to abort goes against all they believe, **against what they**

would do if life circumstances were different. But, she had a choice, and it saved her life.

Our choices were very different, but the truth is, I felt the same things as her; grief and anger for the way my life would change, and for making it more difficult to leave the toxicity. So, I was proud of her, for her strength, the courage to put her family and herself first, and for taking on the burden of her choice to keep those around her above the poverty level.

It is funny how two different choices can evoke the same emotions. I am thankful we each had a choice, because I do not know where we would be if we didn't. We have to keep fighting for the right to choose, fighting to teach understanding of the whys, and fighting to help all those who need support, love and a helping hand, regardless of their choice.

MY HEALTHCARE TEAM SAVED ME

My husband and I really wanted a baby. We were in our mid-thirties. We'd been trying for a year. I got pregnant. We were ecstatic. I quickly started experiencing debilitating morning sickness, constantly wrenching, vomiting, dry heaving all day, all night. Smelling food, seeing food on tv shows, and typing emojis of food made me vomit, even if there was nothing in my stomach. It continued for over six weeks, over forty-two days. I couldn't work, I didn't sleep, I could barely stand up. I cried throughout every day, praying for the misery to pass. At 12 weeks pregnant, my medical team told me I was experiencing a **"missed miscarriage."** There was no living baby in my uterus, but my body didn't register that and continued acting as though it were pregnant.

I now had a few options – v if my body would finally recognize the failed pregnancy and evict the knotted mass of cells it was forming in my uterus, or take abortion pills, which would prompt an immediate and thorough evacuation. If I chose the first option and my body failed to naturally evict, it would become lethally dangerous, at which point we would have to surgically remove the uterine occupants or take the abortion pills.

"Wait and see" would mean days upon days of continued agony, misery, and pain for me.

I wanted it to end. The pills cost me $4. I didn't wait.

I threw up all day long, as usual. I took the pills, and then my body started violently aborting. And then, like a true miracle, I wasn't nauseous anymore. My uterus and my poor stomach and acid-burned esophagus started to recover. I could eat. I could smell! I could sleep and stand and walk.

I mourned. But throughout the recovery process, I was eternally grateful for that quick and easy release — that I could take this magnificent little pill and help my heart and body start to heal. Science was miraculous for me and my experience. My healthcare team saved me. I got pregnant again later that year. My daughter is almost three, very healthy and fun and funny. That pregnancy was not easy, but not nearly as debilitating as my first. I'll always be thankful for the quick and thorough care I received. I don't like to remember the experience, but the point is, I'm still here to remember it. I'm alive and healthy and I have a future to look forward to.

WHATEVER HAPPENED NEXT WAS MY CHOICE

If the Led Zeppelin box set was the soundtrack to the awakening of my own body during my late teens,, a heady mix of sweat and Drakkar Noir cologne was the scent. I'm not ashamed to say that I enjoyed sex — **like really enjoyed sex** — as a teenage girl. Part of it was the pure physical pleasure in my recently changed body, and part of it was the attention from boys and the control I could exert with — and over — my own body.

When I was barely 18, in the last semester of high school, already dreaming of running away to my new life in college, I spent a lusty and lovely night with a sweet boy in my class. We were careful, we thought, and young and dumb and exploring how our bodies could fit together. Without even taking a test, I knew we'd made a mistake, and found out I was pregnant a few weeks later. This boy was kind and supportive. He knew innately that whatever happened next was my choice because it was my body.

I called a Planned Parenthood clinic to make an appointment, and we crowdsourced funds from our friends to cover the expenses. I felt nothing but relief after I had a safe abortion at a clinic near Boston. I have looked back so many times and thanked whatever stars aligned that let me be alive as a pregnant teenager in that time and place — those stars that let me have control of my own life's path, especially so early in my journey.

PRO-LIFE V. PRO-CONTROL

I am a privileged white woman. I am happily married and have three healthy sons. My husband has had a vasectomy, and we do not want any more children. If I found myself pregnant at this time in my life, close to 40 — I would not wish to continue the pregnancy. I repeat — I am a happily married woman with no desire to have more children, and although I could afford to raise another child, I have no desire to do so.

I have health insurance, a husband that provides well for our family, and the support of extended family who would love and help with another baby. *I repeat: I do not want another child.*

This country is full of women from all walks of life who are unable to financially, physically, or emotionally care for a child. This disproportionately affects women of color who do not have the same access to health care and, for many reasons, are not able to afford a child or have the support of others to raise that child. We are not a pro-life country when we force a woman to birth a child that she is unable to care for. We do not offer that woman financial, physical, or emotional support. There is absolutely nothing pro-life about that situation. It is forced birth and nothing else.

Rich white men politicians will always find a way for their mistresses to abort. They are not pro-life in any sense of the word. They want power over women, it's as simple as that. Anyone "pro-life" would support gun control, access to safe abortions, universal healthcare, LGBTQIA+ rights, and police reform. Anything less is pro-control.

I have every advantage in this world and will not have another pregnancy. That is my right over my own body. For those with no support and no system on their side, we must continue to fight.

I CAN'T WORK THROUGH ANOTHER PREGNANCY

When I was 32, after having my two daughters and numerous failed pregnancies, I had an abortion. My husband and I knew that we were done having kids and the potential of further heartbreak from miscarriage. Our youngest was 1 year old. The day I found out I was pregnant, I had taken our cat to the vet after acting weird for a few days. She died mysteriously later that day. The next day I drove to Soldotna with a supportive mom friend. I mourned the loss of my beloved adventure cat, the loss of my previous pregnancies, and felt the panic of being pregnant when I already was at my mental capacity. Thoughts ran through my head: "I'm a bad mother" , "I can't work through another pregnancy", "Where would a new baby even go in our house???" The people at Planned Parenthood were so kind. They asked no invasive questions. The process was smooth and I have no regrets. Yesterday at my well-woman visit I found out that the Planned Parenthood I went to is now closed, a year later. Today I mourn for all the women on the Peninsula who now need to go to Anchorage to access an abortion. A pill I literally took in an office, will now take hours for women to access.

FOR FUCK'S SAKE, NO ONE LIKES GETTING AN ABORTION

My heart still pounds and races when I think of 22-year-old me, nearly two decades ago, who stared at the stick with the two lines, my breasts tender, nervously chain-smoking, calling my best friend for some kind of magic advice.

I was in grad school from a middle class white family, and given all the sex education and birth control options in the world. I had a family that probably would have swooped in and provided financial or logistical support for a new baby.

But...

This child was conceived drunk with a former abuser of mine. The relationship was... complicated... although consensual (I know, I know). He lived in a different state. His family was very religious and rife with alcoholism and abuse. His mother had been adopting children lately, and he assured me that if she found out about this baby, she would do anything in her power to make sure it ended up with her.

Even after that day with the pink stick, the calls, the tears, and the terror of not knowing what to do... I drank. Like a fish. Like I always did when I didn't know how to deal with life or make a decision. Did I drink to excuse ending the pregnancy? **Maybe.** Did I drink because I had a problem that was out of my control? **Likely.** Did I truly believe having an abortion was the easy way out and needed to be atoned for? **A little bit.**

I went to a clinic in San Diego and had a less-than-positive experience. I was deeply shamed by the Planned Parenthood counselor for not "appreciating the risks this doctor took to provide me with services." Well, I guess current events make that more true than ever, but it certainly didn't feel good at the time.

You'll notice I referred to this pregnancy as a child. I believe I can be pro-choice and mourn the potential life that could have been. I can be pro-choice and still know that my mental health and decision-making processes led to unsafe sex and a "situation" that could have been avoided. I can be brutally honest and tell you now, sixteen years clean and sober, that as a mother by CHOICE of three amazing children — no one should be forced to carry and deliver and care for a new life. The burden is too great.

Perhaps that child would have been ok; maybe the responsibility of birthing a new and unique little soul into this world was the event that could have gotten me sober. Perhaps that child would have thrived in my care and not gotten all the ACEs that I feared it would. I can never know the answer to these kinds of questions, but every time I read about a baby left to die outside in a hot car while mama is in a dope house, or a child locked in an animal crate so that mom can turn tricks, my stomach sinks, my heart hurts, and I cry tears of GRATITUDE that one less unwanted child was given to this world.

I still love and talk to that little baby that wasn't meant to come to me at that time or place. I mourn all the women in this position because as a friend said it so well, "For fuck's sake, no one *likes* having an abortion." I live in the grey area of knowing this was the absolute right choice for me, and realizing I have moral and ethical sticky feelings about it. If it were purely a medical procedure, it wouldn't have the emotional or spiritual weight it does. It wouldn't have the secrecy or shame. I still don't know if I should wear this proudly or quietly some days. But all days, I wear it. And I am truly thankful for that.

I TOOK THE MEDICATION WITH MY MOTHER BY MY SIDE

I was 26 years old. I had recently launched my own company. I had only recently begun to develop trust and in my ability to understand myself. I was invited to a house party by friends. I met this guy, and we clicked immediately! He was attractive, smart, had his own business, and shared many of my interests. He was also very charming. I believed I had discovered a new love interest.

Although I wouldn't normally do it on the first night, we ended up hooking up because it was so magical and there was booze involved. It was great drunk sex. As we said our goodbyes in the morning, we made a few impromptu plans to meet up and do something later.

When I texted him later, he informed me he couldn't hang because he had a girlfriend! WTF?! Why didn't that come up? At least before he had sex with me. He was lying to me and to her.

A few weeks later, anytime I ate or smelled food, I started to feel sick. A pregnancy test revealed I was indeed pregnant. If I decided to retain the child, my mother assured me she would be there to support me and assist me in raising it. I realized how much my life and her life would be influenced by my decision. I called him and informed him of my pregnancy. He sent me cash for an abortion and said not to call him ever again.

I had the good fortune to be able to take time off work and use a vehicle to travel to Soldotna to receive a consultation for an abortion. The male doctor accused me of utilizing abortion as a punch card method

of birth control. I informed him, "This is my first and hopefully last abortion. I'm a serial monogamous person and I wasn't using birth control at the time." I found it hard to comprehend that, after finally deciding to get an abortion, the doctor was now insulting me. He did apologize.

I was fortunate to be pregnant early enough to use the abortion pill, preventing the need for him to operate on me.

At my best friend's place, I took the medication with my mother by my side. They supported me throughout the abortion and looked after me the following several days. I made time to sit down and hold a ceremony for the fetus where lots of my emotions were felt and accepted.

I appreciate the choice I made. I love the life that I'm living now. I'm grateful I was able to have a choice. I'm grateful for all the women and men who battled to legalize abortion in the past.

IT WAS NICE BUT DIDN'T LAST

My husband didn't want to have kids, and I thought I was okay with that. I had a lot of things to fill my life, and I loved him. Then one night, switching between birth control options, we weren't quite as careful as we should have been — just one night. And then I was late. I doubted I was pregnant, but I couldn't stop thinking about it, so I left work, drove to CVS, brought a pregnancy test back to the office, and sat in the bathroom, just waiting the sixty seconds to ease my mind. It came back positive. I knew at that moment that I wanted the baby. I have always believed in the right to choose, but I knew what I was going to choose. Life went on; I had a beautiful baby girl, and her dad stepped up to the challenge, but things change, relationships fracture, and now, years later, I find myself going through a divorce as Roe v. Wade is overturned.

As I navigated through the separation, I had another brief romantic entanglement. It was nice but didn't last. We were safe, and I had no reason for concern until I was ten days late. I weighed all the variables and thought it was incredibly unlikely I was pregnant, but after ten days, my mind was spiraling down a worrisome path. Again, I left work, drove to CVS to buy a pregnancy test, and sat in the bathroom at my office, waiting for lines to appear on a little white stick. This time, it was different. I was going through a divorce and already had one child I was worried about ruining. I didn't want to start all over again. The man I'd slept with had moved onto a different phase in his life, and I couldn't imagine reaching out to tell him I was pregnant. I never thought I would get an abortion, but as I sat in that bathroom, the day after Roe v. Wade was overturned, I thought I was lucky that I probably could still get one, if I needed to, for a little while anyway. And I would have. The test was negative. My period came the next day. Everything back to status quo. But I will never

presume to know what I could, or would, or will do.

Life is a series of complicated decisions we have to make for ourselves. To live fully, we need the ability to make those choices, the easy ones and the hard ones. I've always known this, but it hit me differently, as I wrapped my pregnancy test carefully in a paper towel and buried it in the trash can, to avoid starting office gossip. No hard decisions for me today, but I don't know about tomorrow. And I hope that when my daughter is older and is faced with her own complicated decisions, whatever those may be, that she'll live in a country that protects her right to make them.

"When we women offer our experience as our truth, as human truth, all the maps change. There are new mountains."

— Ursula K. Le Guin

———— ● ————

I FELL PREGNANT AGAIN SEVEN MONTHS LATER

I was only 23; just started my first "big girl" job. I was engaged, but my fiancé was involved in an unpaid apprenticeship. My god, we were so poor. I found out I was pregnant right around 5 weeks. All I kept thinking was, "I don't want people to be disappointed in me. I should have been smarter." In all actuality, I was on the pill. Just a statistical BC pregnancy, I guess. But I knew my parents would be disappointed. I had a wedding to be in six months down the road and thought my friends would be so angry that I couldn't participate in normal wedding festivities if I was pregnant. We were 13 states away from all support systems. I truly felt I couldn't keep that baby.

It took me a few weeks to gather the money for the procedure. I was 7 weeks pregnant when I took the little pills, and I sat in my house and bawled for two days while cramping, bleeding, and passing the sack. It's what I wanted at the time, but it mentally wrecked me. Our relationship suffered, I felt I had robbed a little life. I felt like I had robbed us of an alternate future. However, I can't say 100% that I wish I had kept the pregnancy.

Still using the same birth control pill I did for years, I fell pregnant again seven months later. **What the fuck.** I kept him, and he's a thriving 8-year-old boy who I never could imagine my life without. If I had kept the first pregnancy, I would have never had him. It's been nine years since that happened and I still think every day of my decision. Who would that baby have been? Was it a boy or a girl? Would we have been able to scrape by if I kept it? Were the years of secondary infertility I had after my son some sort of karmic revenge on my abortion? I'll never have answers.

Regardless of my own mental anguish, I'm thankful every day for the

LEGAL services I received. I was prepped by an amazing medical staff at Planned Parenthood. They called me to check in on me. They offered me counseling services. I cannot imagine women being put in the position I was and having to seek a back door abortion. Women will die.

Thanks for giving me a platform. I've only told a few close friends. It feels nice to not feel so alone.

WE KNEW WE WOULD BRING THIS CHILD INTO THE WORLD

It's almost 1:00 am here and I'm wide awake after cleaning up the vomit-filled bed of my 8-year-old. I'm also pregnant with my third child and my fourth pregnancy; A child we've chosen to keep. Our parent game was on lockdown with our family for four, or so we thought.

When we found out, my husband and I simultaneously cried and celebrated. We knew we would bring this child into this world if the signs continued to point to "Yes." We had a choice, and we didn't feel burdened by that choice. This decision was not unknown to us.

In our early 20s, almost twenty years ago, we were met with the same decision, **except we were not ready to start a family.** We made the choice to end the pregnancy.

We made an appointment at the local Planned Parenthood. We had to walk through protesters yelling at us that we were killing our baby. At 23, I felt that. I wholeheartedly felt like I had given away my one chance to be a mother.

The fucking shit storm that followed was awful. The doctors were kind. The staff was supportive. My health insurance even paid for the procedure. Talk about privilege, right?! But that day, I felt like my soul was sucked out of me. I vomited everywhere during the procedure. My now husband (then-boyfriend) waited nervously in the waiting room. We left, myself sobbing; he was lost on how to console me. We went out to lunch. What the fuck! This was the beginning of a long, hard journey learning about myself, my emotions, years of trauma around sexuality, and undoing years of suppressed emotional trauma. I grew up that day. I had a choice, and it was difficult.

I think how our life would be different, as neither of us had solid careers. We were piss poor post-college kids, and I was preparing to head to graduate school that fall. Maybe this third child we are about to have in our late thirties is bringing our broken hearts and story full circle — despite knowing my own daughters may not have that same choice in their life as I did in mine.

THE SOUND OF THAT HEARTBEAT CEMENTED MY FAITH

My husband was out of town for the day of my scheduled check-up.

Home with our firstborn (via emergency cesarean), I was well into my second trimester. I was wearing a few maternity outfits.

We had heard the heartbeat at our last visit.

This was a big deal for us.

I had lost two pregnancies early on over the last year, one in December ~*Christa*, and one in the Easter season ~*Easta*

We chose to wait before going in for a check-up this time around. The sound of that heartbeat cemented my faith.

On the day of my appointment, I joyfully made ready for our trip to town, just me and our 3-year-old.

It was all smiles and curious questions until the new midwife attending to me could not find the heartbeat.

She was new, she must be mistaken. That is all I could believe.

Our sweet 3-year-old and I were sent to the hospital for a sonogram.

There was no heartbeat.

I was told to go home, it would be two days before I could have an extraction done.

The sadness that engulfed me before paled in comparison to the depth of loss I felt on this day.

~*Aaron*, the dream, the hope, the plan, was no more.

It was July 2, 1998, the day the Icicle Seafoods building burned down.

Clouds of ammonia were stopping traffic, my dearest friend finally made it to our house, and **pulled me off of my floor — manically scrubbing.** She arrived with pizza for our children and precious hugs for me.

The loss, mentally and physically, took time to heal from.

Much time.

I have scars.

In December of 1999 I gave natural birth to our second child.

I still list five pregnancies when asked on admitting forms.

Each conception altered my dreams, my cells, my heart, and they will never be forgotten.

I remember — I do not count my tubal pregnancy because I had not "felt" pregnant. My dreams had not been seeded....

But it is July 2022, and today it is possible that an extraction for that very painful and dangerous conception may not be available in many parts of our world.

MY BODY BELONGED TO ME AGAIN

I had an abortion when I was a senior in high school in the early 2000s. As a woman, it was a terrible time to come of age, because our bodies didn't belong to us. Our bodies belonged to all the boys who told us they loved us while they pressured us, deceived us, and encouraged us to become incoherent so we gave them less resistance. Our bodies and those practices were being marketed to these boys on a continuous loop of late-night television commercials that reinforced this behavior. **Our bodies could be purchased for $9.99 and included a bonus DVD.**

Consent was implied by existing in their spaces. Rape was subjective, and when it inevitably happened under these circumstances, it was your fault because you were there.

I wasn't given a choice to conceive that night because I wasn't conscious. I wasn't even given a choice to make a bad choice. Choice was only afforded to me in the aftermath, and I was steadfast in my decision.

I watched as disapproval of me grew on the faces of those in my circle. I was acutely aware of the sympathy they gave to the rapist when he announced he didn't want me to abort his baby, because "He should have a say."

I never wavered, and in the nineteen years since, I have never once regretted my choice… because the day that I was finally allowed to have a say in what happened to my body was the day my body belonged to me again.

BECAUSE IT WAS THE RIGHT THING FOR ME

There's this photo from a time when my then-husband was out fishing and I was, simply put, not okay. My body was broken in many ways after a difficult birth, and I was absolutely drowning in the overwhelm of new motherhood. I was still bleeding and couldn't **"just stop doing so much,"** as my medical providers suggested. My younger sister was moving away, as did my sister-in-law at the time, my mother-in-law tragically passed away just before, my own mom was thousands of miles away, and I felt devastatingly alone in my responsibility to be the matriarch providing for my commercial fishing family in all the ways women are culturally expected to in Kodiak.

This photo of my former father-in-law with my daughter, was taken right after a chiropractor appointment. He had met me there and watched Eliza for me, just sitting in the truck, so they could be nearby just in case they needed me. He was the reason why I could finally get a little space, just an hour-long appointment, to focus on caring for myself. I was desperate. I can't adequately describe how helpless I felt needing him to do that for me, which he did so easily and eagerly. I realize now there were many more people I could have asked for help from, but couldn't and didn't, but that doesn't take away my immense gratitude for Bill on this day and every other.

I dreamt of having children. And then having gone through it once, immediately resolved not to have any more. Not because it was the right thing for my family, but because it was the right thing for me and I had the right to say, "No. No more." I was shamed for it. My decision is partially responsible for the end of that marriage, but I'm still grateful that I had the right and the opportunity to say no.

And I am mourning for so many women who won't be able to.

NOT READY TO MAKE
THIS COMMITMENT

When I was in college, after a spell of indiscriminate sex partners who were not at all interesting or good to me, I met an artist who had traveled the world. I fell in love for the first time. This man stayed in town with me for a few months and then moved back home, which broke my heart.

After he left town in the middle of winter, my roommates also moved out, leaving me to pay the rent for our tiny house on my own. I couldn't afford to pay for everything and turned down the heat to save money. **I remember waking up in the morning that winter and seeing my breath.** At some point, my lover's best friend came over and spent the night with me. We listened to the harp and flute, and fell into bed together.

I moved in with him because we were both broke and needed to pay rent. The first place was in his basement. Then we moved into a ratty second-floor apartment above an abandoned downtown storefront. We had separate bedrooms and did not sleep together all the time, at least not at first. **We made art, food, and sunshine together. I felt whole for the first time since I was young.** We did have sex and when we did, it was great. And when I missed my period for the first time since I started having them, I took a pregnancy test, which was positive. We were both 24 years old.

When I told him I was pregnant, he was very serious. We talked about our possible futures. We were both in college and both very poor. He acknowledged he was not ready to raise a child and not ready to be a father.

I acknowledged that having a child at this point in my life would lead to a whole host of changes: ostracization from my parents, a sudden shift in my education and career plans, and a shift from expansion and exploration to parenthood, which I knew would mean a dedication to raising a little human to adulthood probably on my own. I was not ready to make this commitment, and neither was he.

So. We scheduled an appointment with a doctor who agreed to perform an abortion for us. We scheduled this as soon as we found out, which couldn't have been more than 5 weeks into this pregnancy. My boyfriend accompanied me to all the appointments and could not have been a kinder, gentler supporter of this decision.

The doctor was so kind. He was older, and explained exactly what he was going to do with both of us in the room. He was going to insert a plug of some kind of seaweed into my cervix, which would gradually absorb moisture over the next 24 hours and gently dilate the opening. He sent us home with instructions to come back the next day for the curettage. My boyfriend waited for me and took me home afterwards. There was little to no pain, and we were both relieved.

There was some worry about the loss of the little child we had made together. We had a mutual friend who was kind of witchy and sweet. Her belief was that the soul of a child didn't enter the body until it knew it was wanted. And if it had to wait til later on, it would return when the timing was better. This helped us get through our somber grieving immensely.

HAVING A THIRD CHILD WOULD HAVE CHANGED EVERYTHING

My husband and I already had two beautiful, healthy children well into self-sufficient ages. Two children were all we could afford, and all we were planning to have. At the time, I was the only one working and fully supporting our family of four. I had just started my own business, so the income was meager, and we didn't have insurance, but we were getting by. **It seems society has this impossible expectation of women to work as if we don't have children and to mother as if we don't have work.** And so many of us are doing both — working and mothering. It is exhausting to try and do it all, and I often feel as if I am failing at everything, with never enough hours on any day.

Since we were content as a family of four, we planned for him to get a vasectomy so I could get off birth control. Unfortunately, our order of operations was off. I jumped the gun on stopping birth control, so we went back to using condoms. He kept procrastinating on making the vasectomy appointment. One passionate evening, after an extended time apart, we didn't grab a condom. That evening resulted in a third, unplanned and unwanted pregnancy.

Having a third child would have changed everything; the life we had built and the life we still dreamt of. After considering all of our options and the myriad of factors, we made the decision to have an abortion. My husband fully supported the decision. He honored that it was my body and my choice.

He went with me to all the appointments, but I still felt very alone and so much shame. During the days between the positive pregnancy test and taking the abortion pill, he was the only one who knew. He was "there for me," but only as much as a man can be. He finally made the overdue appointment to get the vasectomy.

While I do not regret my decision to get an abortion, I often wonder how our lives would be different had we chosen otherwise. I wonder who that mass of cells might have become. Annually, I recognize both the expected due date and the date of my abortion. They are moments in the cycle of each year that always give me pause and intense emotions.

Since my abortion, I have shared my story with a couple of close friends. It has been healing to talk about my experience finally. Only when I began to share did I realize that many women have had their own and similar experiences. The shame and stigma around abortion are so isolating. I hope that as more women share their stories, we can overcome that stigma and begin to heal. I know my healing continues as I share my story through this project — though my healing intermingles with rage and heartbreak. I feel rage when I acknowledge that my daughter is coming of age in a world where she has less choice and bodily autonomy than the generations before her.

I am heartbroken that she will have to consider the status of reproductive rights when making decisions about higher education or travels after high school. The journey to get back to where we were will be long and arduous. Luckily there is strength in numbers, and I know my daughter will be by my side, just as I will be by hers, along with many others passionate about being on the right side of this moment in history.

THE SAME WOMAN WHO COUNSELED ME FOR MY ABORTION DELIVERED MY PERFECT BABY BOY

I knew I was pregnant. That's not why I made an appointment at the Family Planning clinic. It wasn't my first time in this situation, crying, pregnant, sitting there with the kind woman who could not change the wild night a few weeks ago, or that I took Plan B a day too late. The first time I had sat in that office, with the confirmation pregnancy test clearly showing the big pink plus, I knew what I wanted. That clarity was comfort, in a way. The one-night stand with the person whose name I can't recall was not the introduction to motherhood I wanted for myself. That decision was easy, and for me, the process of scheduling and self-managing the medical abortion was relatively easy too.

It was harder the second time. Another unexpected positive test due to another careless night and a careless week after when Plan B could have worked. **But now I was married, and crying at the clinic.** I was crying because it was the only place where I would be given the care and information I needed to make the right choice for myself. I had drunk alcohol between the conception night and taking the pregnancy test... would keeping the pregnancy unnecessarily bring a damaged child into the world, or should I end it now? I was in my upper thirties, "geriatric" according to the OBGYN terminology, and at increased risk of having a child with genetic abnormalities, which I wasn't willing to handle. I needed abortion as a choice on the table, but this time the choice was excruciating.

Nine months later, the same woman who counseled

me and referred me for my abortion delivered my perfect baby boy. A baby boy who would not exist, and who would not be loved and cared for in the way I can offer him now, if not for the choices I've had.

"It is terrifying to people when women step up

and start owning the story that they have not

owned. And I'm seeing so much of this,

and it is a seismic shift."

— AMANDA PALMER

———— • ————

CONTRIBUTORS

Terrified I Wouldn't Recognize My Own Child
Thank You, Meredith

They Had to Sedate Her
Thank you, Jasmine

The Death of a Future I Thought I Was Going to Have
Thank you, Red

Discovering Who I Am Again
Can I See Your Vagina?
Momma Held It Down
Thank you, Savanna

It Was a Shock to Me
Abortion was Illegal in My State
Thank you, Kimberly

For Fuck's Sake, No One Likes Getting an Abortion
Thank you, Angela

One, Two, Three, Four, Five
Thank you, Amanda

Whatever Happened Next Was My Choice
Thank you, Carly

WRITE A MOMOLOGUE

The project builds community for *all who identify with mothering*. Feel welcome to explore the more unconventional edges of Motherhood and share stories that validate and lift this community.

Submit yours at www.MomologueCollective.com

GLOSSARY

ACEs – Adverse Childhood Experiences: How various forms of physical and emotional abuse, neglect, and household dysfunction relate to children's developmental risk, and how the association is mediated through mothers' depressive symptoms and fair/poor health.

Anencephaly – A severe congenital condition in which a large part of the skull is absent along with the cerebral hemispheres of the brain.

Bili Lights – Bili Lights are a type of light therapy (phototherapy) that is used to treat newborn jaundice.

Cesarean (C-section) – The surgical delivery of a baby through a cut (incision) made in the mother's abdomen and uterus.

Cerclage – A treatment that involves temporarily sewing the cervix closed with stitches. This may help prevent preterm birth in some cases.

Clomid – Clomiphene is used to induce ovulation (egg production) in women who do not produce ova (eggs) but wish to become pregnant.

CPAP – Continuous Positive Airway Pressure: A means of providing respiratory support to a new born child with either upper airway obstruction or respiratory failure.

Curettage – Is a procedure to remove tissue from inside a uterus. Health care providers perform dilation and curettage to diagnose and treat certain uterine conditions — such as heavy bleeding — or to clear the uterine lining after a miscarriage or abortion.

D&C – Dilation and Curettage: The most common method of early abortion. This method is simple and considered one of the safest ways to end an early pregnancy. A D&C procedure is routine, considered safe and does not affect the ability to get pregnant in the future.

Effacement – Effacement refers to the thinning of the cervix during labor.

Estrogen – Estrogens are a group of hormones that play an important role in the normal sexual and reproductive development in women. They are also sex hormones.

Femara – Letrozole (Femara) Letrozole lowers estrogen production which can be used to induce ovulation in patients with irregular ovulation patterns or those who suffer from anovulation. It can also help to increase egg production in women who ovulate normally but have unexplained infertility.

HCG trigger shots – A trigger shot usually containing a hormone called human chorionic gonadotropin, or HCG, used in fertility therapy.

HELLP – Hemolysis, Elevated Liver enzymes and Low Platelets: A life-threatening pregnancy syndrome usually considered to be a variant of preeclampsia. Both conditions usually occur during the later stages of pregnancy, or soon after childbirth.

IUI – Intrauterine insemination: This type of artificial insemination is a procedure for treating infertility. Sperm that have been washed and concentrated are placed directly in the uterus around the time an ovary releases one or more eggs to be fertilized.

IVF – In vitro fertilization: This is one of the more widely known types of assisted reproductive technology (ART). IVF works by using a combination of medicines and surgical procedures to help sperm fertilize an egg and help the fertilized egg implant in the uterus.

Methotrexate – A type of medicine that stops cells from dividing. It can be used as a way (other than surgery) to treat a pregnancy that has implanted outside the uterus (ectopic pregnancy).

Misoprostol – Used for a medication abortion, medical management of miscarriage, induction of labor, cervical ripening before surgical procedures, and the treatment of postpartum hemorrhage. Due to its wide-ranging applications in reproductive health, misoprostol is on the World Health Organization Model List of Essential Medicines.

OB – Obstetrics or obstetrician: a physician who cares for pregnant people and their babies during pregnancy and childbirth.

Omphalocele – Omphalocele (pronounced uhm-fa-lo-seal) is a birth defect of the abdominal wall. The infant's intestines, liver, or other organs stick outside of the belly through the belly button. The organs are covered in a thin, nearly transparent sac that hardly ever is open or broken.

PPA – Postpartum Anxiety: While PPD (see below) may cause tears and hopelessness, PPA is marked by fears, obsessive concerns, scary thoughts and irritability. Mothers with PPA often experience obsessive behaviors and intrusive thoughts that are disturbing, unwanted, and out-of-character.

PPD – Postpartum Depression: A commonly occuring medical condition characterized by strong feelings of sadness, anxiety and tiredness after giving birth, or being pregnant. These feelings can make it hard to take care of the mother's self and their baby.

Preeclampsia – Preeclampsia is a complication of pregnancy characterized by high blood pressure and high levels of protein in urine that may indicate kidney damage or other signs of organ damage.

Progesterone – Progesterone is a hormone released by the ovaries.

Changing progesterone levels can contribute to abnormal menstrual periods and menopausal symptoms.

Profusion – Is the passage of blood, a blood substitute, or other fluid through the blood vessels or other natural channels in an organ or tissue.

Pneumothorax – A pneumothorax (noo-moe-THOR-aks) is a collapsed lung. A pneumothorax occurs when air leaks into the space between the lung and chest wall and pushes on the outside of the lung and makes it collapse. A pneumothorax can be a complete lung collapse or a collapse of only a portion of the lung.

RPL – Recurrent Pregnancy Loss: A condition when a woman has two or more clinical pregnancy losses (miscarriages) before the pregnancies reach 20 weeks. Losses are classified by when they occur. Loss of a "clinical pregnancy" is diagnosed by a health-care provider using ultrasound.

Saline Histogram – A procedure to evaluate the uterus and the shape of the uterine cavity.

VBAC – Vaginal birth after cesarean.

Vasopressors – A drug that healthcare providers use to make blood vessels constrict or become narrow in people with low blood pressure. Often, these are people in shock who are unable to get enough blood to their vital organs. Without oxygen-rich blood, organs can't function, which can be fatal.

NOTES

www.ingramcontent.com/pod-product-compliance
Lightning Source LLC
Chambersburg PA
CBHW020240130626
46549CB00005B/1978